The Totally Unfoi Herdwick War

or

20/20 Visions

or

More Cumbrian Tales

H. G. Wills

ARTHUR H. STOCKWELL LTD
Torrs Park, Ilfracombe, Devon, EX34 8BA
Established 1898
www.ahstockwell.co.uk

British Library Cataloguing-in-Publication Data.
A catalogue record for this book is available
from the British Library.

By the same author:
The Best Kept Secrets of the Western Marches
Room 22 Revisited
In the Eye of Storms
The Canticle of Rollo Pecorino Bernardosa

ISBN 978-0-7223-5085-0
Printed in Great Britain by
Arthur H. Stockwell Ltd
Torrs Park   Ilfracombe
Devon EX34 8BA

CONTENTS

ACKNOWLEDGEMENTS

What can one say? Although not of the same intellectual calibre as their brothers and sisters of the fells of the Lake District and Pennines, I should like to thank the sheep of Dartmoor for their contributions with regard to Ovian folklore. They too knew of Droopy Drawers, although goodness knows how and why.

It would be remiss of me not to thank Ken Fryer for his knowledge of the route taken by Henry VI and his insistence of walking every foot of the way – hence proving the mind-boggling and astoundingly accurate theories of Annony Mouse, the irony monger of Wigton Road.

With regard to any written proof as to where Henry VI might have travelled to or stayed on his journey around Cumbria in 1464–65, none surely now exist. Lancastrian hosts, at the time, would surely have destroyed any evidence for, as Sir John Harrington, Queen Elizabeth I's 'saucy godson' and an inventor of an early flush toilet during the reign of James I, would have later pointed out, "Treason never prospers. . . ."

As to sanctuary afforded by any of the ecclesiastical houses en route, any written evidence would have been placed unread on the bonfires lit by Thomas Cromwell's louts during the English Reformation in the late 1530s, as they stripped the lead off the rooves of monasteries. Perhaps there are letters or other documents in the Vatican Library which could shed some light on the subject . . . but only time will tell . . . and, up to this point in time, an ominous silence prevails.

H. G. Wills, 3 September 2020.

ILLUSTRATIONS

Xavier the Frog.

INTRODUCTION

The Herdwick War wasn't the least bit unforgettable at all. In fact, most members of the species *Homo sapiens* weren't even aware that it had taken place, because they were in lockdown. Humanity, in early 2020, blinked, and in that instant the misfortunes affecting the Herdwicks and Swaledales of Cumbria occurred and were just as quietly resolved.

In Wiggonby College, that haven of academic tranquillity, life during this period went on as usual. The staff, being mostly members of the species *Ovo bipedus* – and thus imbued with genetic immunity to the virus – were exempt from all restrictions.

However, nothing is entirely free of consequences, as Professor Tethra Hardwick was about to find out on one particular morning. He had intended to enjoy an extended lie-in, but was roused from his slumber by a nightmarish howling – like the mournful bleating of ewes after their lambs had been taken off to market – but multiplied by a factor of hundreds, if not thousands.

Stumbling to the window and drawing apart the curtains, his eyes fell upon a sea of cornflower-blue tail-coated soldiers. They were also adorned in white gilets and knee breeches, as well as black shakos and gaiters. Before him was a brigade of Napoleon's finest – deployed in massive columns, each with a golden-eagle-topped 'Drapeau Tricolore' flapping at its head.

As one they roared repeatedly, *"Vive, l'Empereur! Vive, l'Empereur! Vive, l'Empereur!"*

"Well, you don't see that every day," Tethra couldn't resist saying aloud.

"No, actually you don't!" Chibb Swaledale, his PA, replied.

He had entered the room unannounced, carrying a small silver tray bearing a highly decorated calling card on which were written three words in the best copperplate script: 'Xavier the Frog'.

General de Brigade, Xavier Hippolyte de Grenouille.

CHAPTER 1 – SOUTHER FELL

As Tethra examined the card, Chibb Swaledale began dropping pins one at a time on to the silver tray – which clearly the Professor heard.

"Please stop doing that – it is most annoying!"

"You really don't pay me enough, Professor," Chibb whispered, and he nodded knowingly towards the window.

The space outside, where only a minute previously had been a brigade of Napoleon Bonaparte's infantry, cheering him at the tops of their voices, was now completely empty. All was now silent – apart from the chirping of a few sparrows.

"They've gone!"

"Quick thinking, Batman! But I wonder if General de Brigade Xavier Hippolyte de Grenouille, whose calling card you're holding, is still waiting to see you downstairs?"

He was, and enjoying one of Tethra's Cuban cigars together with a cup of Colombian coffee and, naturally, a glass of Napoleon brandy.

"*Bonjour*," he said without even glancing at his host.

"And *bonjour* to you, Burt Nemo. I see you've made a name for yourself," Tethra responded knowingly.

"Shall I shoot him now or later, Professor?" Chibb whispered.

"No need for that . . . not just yet!"

Lost for words, Burt Nemo, a former gardener at the college, simply fainted and tumbled from his chair on to the Axminster carpet.

Not long afterwards, Yan and Tan Hardwick, Tethra's sons, arrived at Wiggonby from Monkeyrisedale, or, as it is better known, Mungrisdale, where they now lived.

"We came as quick as we could, Fatha!" they announced in unison.

"How did you get here so quickly?"

11

"Has something happened here too? We're responding to last night's skirmish on Souther Fell."

"What happened?"

"About 2 a.m. all hell broke loose – sheep streaming down the fells in terror, chased by French *sapeurs* wielding felling axes and fusiliers firing Charlvilles at anything that moved, all led by a fiend in a brigadier general's uniform," Yan volunteered.

"It was war . . . pure and simple!" Tan added.

"What on earth is happening? Has the world gone mad?" Professor Hardwick asked his sons after recounting the incident outside the college.

Frank Potts, the librarian, who had in the meantime joined the assembled group, then offered his twopenn'orth.

"Souther Fell has had for centuries a reputation of 'spectral armies' appearing from time to time on its slopes. The first recorded instance was in 1735, when a servant of William Lancaster of nearby Blakehills stated he had seen an army marching along the eastern side of the fell for a whole hour. Two years later William Lancaster and family reported seeing columns of men five ranks deep taking the same route. Again in 1744 around twenty-six witnesses testified to seeing the same thing, but added that the infantry were accompanied by cavalry and supply waggons.

Indeed, another William wrote:

Anon, appears a brave, gorgeous show
Of horsemen-shadows moving to and fro . . .

Silent the visionary warriors go,
Winding in ordered pomp their upward way
Till the last banner of the long array
Had disappeared, and every trace is fled
Of splendour – save the beacon's spiry head
Tipt with eve's latest gleam of burning red.

Wordsworth.

"Yes, come to think of it, Coleridge also wrote something along those lines. Some years later, it was all put down as a premonition of the 1745 Jacobite Rebellion, but it's been quiet since then," mused the Professor.

"Well, I hate to disabuse you, Professor," Frank chipped in again, "but a certain Annony Mouse, the irony monger of Wigton Road, wrote a piece for the *Cumberland News* about a trip he and his father made in the early fifties. They were visiting some farmer friends near Souther Fell when the boy, who wasn't supposed to hear what they were talking about, overheard them whispering about an army of ghosts on the fells above the farm."

With that the group headed for the infirmary, where Sister Knuckles was just about to revive Burt Nemo with her 'Torquemadan specialty massage'. Burt was no longer *en grande tenue*, but dressed in one of those gowns which tie up the back. He seemed relieved to see them – possibly hoping for a stay of treatment.

"Well, Mr Nemo, you have some explaining to do."

"What can I say?" he mumbled.

"The truth!" they all bellowed as one.

"Last evening I was out fell-walking on Souther Fell and stopped near the summit for a coffee, just as the sun dropped behind Blencathra. It was a clear night and the stars were . . ."

"Get on with it!" blurted out Chibb with frustration and an intense desire to get to a punchline.

"Suddenly, a black-hooded figure loomed out from nowhere, whispering something unintelligible in a foreign tongue and I passed out . . . but not before noticing the soldiers chasing the poor sheep."

"And that's all you can remember . . . ?"

"'Fraid so!"

"Well, Burt, you've had a harrowing experience – one worse that watching Dirty Furfy captaining Workington AFC playing the Blue Army in that awful Christmas game of '63. You need something to take your mind off it all. Sister Knuckles . . . he's all yours!"

Minutes later, back in the Professor's office and far out of hearing range of Burt Nemo's screams, the reassembled group of Tethra, Yan and Tan Hardwick, Chibb Swaledale and Frank 'Fuss' Potts looked at each other blankly . . . and mulled over the opening and, as it happened, only military skirmish of the brief Herdwick War.

Professor Tethra Hardwick.

CHAPTER 2 – A GHOST OF A CHANCE

All morning and well into the afternoon news filtered into the college from all points of the compass of apparitions and ghostly sittings in the county. Finally, around teatime, the Professor and Frank Potts came up with a plan. Yan, Tan and Chibb would sally out that evening and collect information from specific sites after sunset. It promised to be a cloudless night with a full moon, so the omens were favourable for good sightings of whatever was going on.

Chibb, hoping to see a Solway Blue-tailed parrot like his beloved Painless, volunteered to head for Grune Point just north of Skinberness and overlooking Moricambe Bay. He arrived in his Morgan Aero two-seater just as the sun dipped behind Criffel – a good two hours after the Solway Bore had swirled by.

Hiding behind a large clump of sea holly, he didn't have long to wait. From Anthorn a yawl, loaded with passengers, was sculled down the Wampool Channel and headed out into the Solway towards Powfoot on the Scottish side. Then, abruptly, the craft capsized and those in the muddy brown water tried to scramble on to the keel. Screams wafted in bursts towards Chibb, who jumped up and ran to the water's edge. It was all over in a trice and there was absolutely nothing he could have done . . . even if what he had seen had been real.

His only other destination was Maryport, a dozen or so miles down the coast, where Frank had promised a sighting of a three-masted slave schooner with rigging tangled with seaweed and tattered sails flapping in the breeze as it headed for its home port . . . but Chibb never got there.

Just over a mile south of Silloth the Morgan's engine gave up the ghost, which was, as it turned out, a very unfortunate turn of phrase.

"The battery's flat – that shouldn't have happened."

Chibb looked around and could just make out a light in the window of a stone building in the next field. As he drew closer, it was clearly a tower surrounded by a curtain wall and moat. Then, as he drew nearer, a pillar of flame shot up from the crenellated top floor, and silhouetted against it was a dark-robed and hooded figure of a man with his arms raised high above his head. He seemed to be shouting incantations, which stopped Chibb in his tracks.

Without warning the tower exploded, bowling over and knocking clean out the college's number-one observer, who awoke next morning shivering and wet with dew. The Morgan started first time, and with a welcome turn of speed Chibb headed back to Wiggonby.

Yan and Tan tossed a coin for the southern and eastern options. Yan won and set off for Keswick. He had one stop to make en route, which involved viewing the 'Bishop of Barfe' – a white-painted rock 700 feet high above Thornthwaite on the south-western shore of Bassenthwaite. It was so highlighted to commemorate the spectacular death of Frederick Augustus Harvey, 4th Earl of Bristol and Bishop of Derry, in 1783.

He had been a rather odd fellow for a prelate of the Church of England, and he had startled George III during one of his sane periods by declaring he was most decidedly an agnostic. He also hailed from an equally eccentric family, of which Voltaire, the French historian and philosopher, had commented that "When God created the human race, he made men, women and Harveys."

His demise at fifty-three years of age is said to have been the result of overindulgence in alcohol, which he had imbibed to excess in The Swan at Thornthwaite. He had boasted that he could ride his horse to the summit of Barfe – some 1,535 feet above the lake – the locals took on the wager. Horse and rider managed 700 feet before tumbling to their deaths. The Bishop was duly buried further down the slope at the site of another white-painted stone, called 'The Clerk'.

Yan was mystified about his mission and was even more astounded to see the spectral figures of horse and rider galloping down the steep slope and plunging into the lake. This was all the more astonishing as the good bishop had in reality died twenty years after his drunken bet. Indeed, he had shuffled off this mortal coil in a shed in the small village of Albano, while en route to Rome – having recently been released after an eighteen-month stretch in the Milan jail for allegedly spying on the invading French Army.

Mulling over the aquatic disappearance of the agnostic bishop, but without coming to any conclusion, Yan continued on to Castlerigg Stone Circle on a flat-topped hill to the south-east of Keswick. The circle is 100 feet in diameter and consists of thirty-eight local stones of volcanic origin – one as tall as seven and a half feet. It had, according to Frank Potts, been erected between 3500 and 1500 BC, in the Late Neolithic to Early Bronze Age. Its function is in some doubt, but it probably had an astronomical function in fixing the dates for gatherings and possible religious rites, rather than dates for sowing and harvesting grain.

Approaching from the north, he parked his souped-up Austin 7 on Castlerigg Brow and walked the rest of the way – keeping to the hedgerow. With half an hour to spare before the setting sun disappeared behind Grasmoor Fell, Yan found a vantage point under a large hawthorn bush. The scene was deserted and a gentle breeze blew down from the north. Everything looked absolutely normal . . . and then gradually images of people began to materialise around the stones. In the centre of the circle, on top of a pile of wood, there appeared to be a wicker cage containing a young naked woman.

Barely audible chanting slowly increased to a low-pitched murmur. A black-robed and hooded figure emerged from nowhere holding on high a blue-flamed burning torch, which he threw on to the woodpile. Instantly, an unholy bonfire roared into flame, engulfing the cage and its terrified occupant. The crowd howled wildly and cavorted erratically around the rim of stone teeth.

Then the priest threw up his arms and all movement ceased. The only sounds now were those of the screaming burning woman. Suddenly, a red shaft of forked lightning stabbed down on to the inferno – and the scene, in the blink of an eye, returned to normal . . . but not before the black-robed figure turned and fixed Yan with a red-eyed stare.

Meanwhile, in the east of the county, Tan tootled along the back lanes on a light-green Lambretta towards Croglin, which for those not in the know is – even now – a small village of no more than twenty houses tucked below the western slopes of the Pennines. It is about eight miles west of Alston and ten miles south of the partially ruined Augustinian priory at Lanercost. If that is of no help it's in the Back of Beyond, approximately twelve miles as the crow flies south-east of the great metropolis of Carlisle.

Despite its relative insignificance it was, as Frank Potts had drummed into Tan, the most grisly spot in the county, and the haunt – no less – of the Croglin Vampire.

Tan was well prepared and equipped with a couple of pints of Newcastle

Brown Ale or 'jungle juice', which had a justifiable reputation on the terraces of St James' Park of being 'holy water'. He also wore a steel collar under his polo-necked sweater, and in his satchel were a hammer and three wooden stakes, which he recalled had been very useful in a film he had seen years earlier in the 'Botchy', starring Christopher Lee.

The Robin Hood was, of course, closed, but Tan had a small map which he had copied from *The Ghostly Guide to the Lake District*. He headed towards the boneyard of St John the Baptist's Church. Searching for the vaulted tomb, which had played a prominent part in the story, he only found headstones. Picking one belonging to two brothers – Tom and Jack Byers – Yan hunkered down with his back against the lichen-encrusted stone.

He couldn't resist a swig of holy water – in fact his second or third – as he went over the story in his mind. According to legend it all began just after the English Civil War (1642–51), which, as Tan kept fortifying himself, sounded like a very sophisticated and civilised afternoon cream tea – but, of course, it wasn't.

In a rented one-storey building called Croglin Low Hall lived the two brothers Cranswell and their sister. It was a hot summer's evening and Miss Cranswell went to bed with the shutters open, but the window closed. She couldn't sleep and absent-mindedly looked out through the window at a small coppice between the church and the farm. Gradually, she became aware of two small red glowing points of light, which appeared to be getting nearer. Abruptly, she discerned they were eyes – the eyes of a stooped figure which began to scratch at the lead around the glass windowpanes with wickedly curved nails at the end of spindly bony fingers. She leapt out of bed, but couldn't turn the key in the bedroom door as her hands were shaking.

One of the panes smashed sending a shower of glass on to the stone floor and in an instant the fiend flipped the latch, vaulted into the room and attacked the screaming girl – pulling her to the floor and biting her neck. The commotion woke her two brothers, who broke down their sister's bedroom door, but the vampire was gone – disappearing into the night without trace.

They all subsequently went on a holiday to the continent to rid their minds of the awful assault . . . but oddly enough returned to the farm that autumn. Nothing happened until the following March, when the same scratching at the window began once more. This time the brothers were ready and chased the creature into the wood. One got off a shot from his pistol and swore he'd hit the beast in the leg, but again the vampire had disappeared without trace.

The next morning the village was in uproar as another girl had been bitten

– this time the daughter of the owner of Croglin High Hall. A massive search ensued and the villagers converged on a large tomb in the centre of the graveyard. Casting caution to the wind, they broke in and found two coffins – one with its lid ajar. Inside was a brown mummified corpse . . . with a bullet wound in one of its legs. There was only one thing to do . . . so the enraged villagers burned the coffin and its contents there and then.

"Quite a story!" Tan whispered under his breath, and then, having emptied the second bottle of holy water, nodded off to sleep . . . only to be woken by the presence of a black-robed and hooded figure standing over him. Tan almost jumped out of his skin, but he couldn't move. The figure just hovered there, looking down at him. Then slowly it drifted away southward and appeared to beckon him to follow . . . before disappearing on the whiff of a gentle breeze blowing from the north.

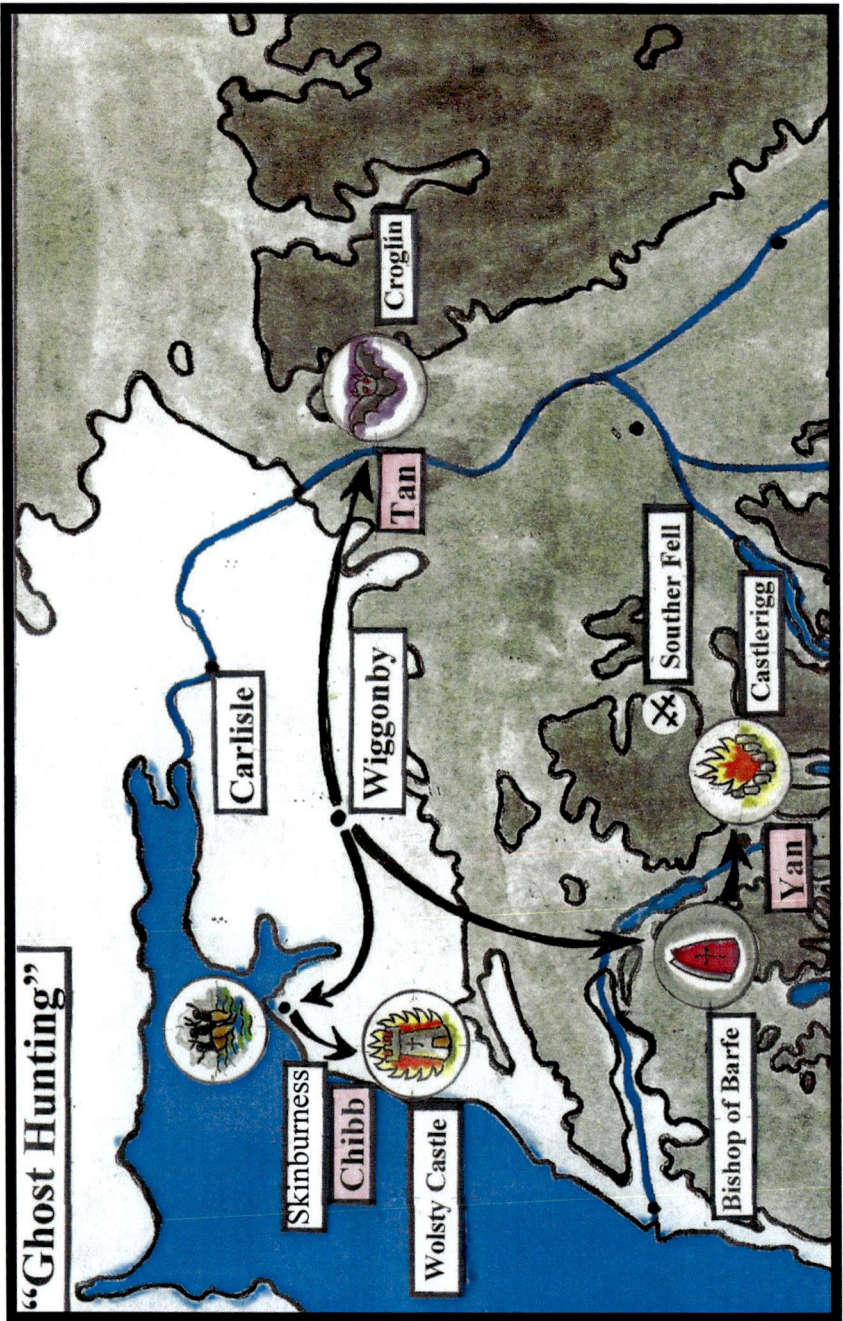

"Ghost Hunting"

Croglin

Tan

Carlisle

Wiggonby

Souther Fell

Castlerigg

Yan

Skinburness

Chibb

Wolsty Castle

Bishop of Barfe

20

CHAPTER 3 – OF CABBAGES AND KINGS

"'The time has come,' the Walrus said."

Tethra Hardwick began somewhat haltingly. He couldn't quite find the words to explain why he and Frank had sent Yan, Tan and Chibb on what had turned out to be three really harrowing experiences.

"Yes, Father, you owe us an explanation for what you put us through," his eldest son intoned.

"Well, Frank and I were very suspicious about the first incident, involving Brigadier General Xavier Hippolyte de Grenouille. The story of the spectral army of Souther Fell is well known . . . but an army of French Soldiers led by former gardener of the college who ended up terrorising Cumbrian sheep couldn't be ignored. Was it an isolated phenomenon or part of something more widespread? So we chose three separate areas for investigation, never suspecting things might get out of hand . . . but, sadly, they did."

Tethra paused to catch his thoughts and then began to give his interpretation of what happened . . . starting with Chibb.

"Runaway couples have been going to Gretna to be married over the anvil for centuries. Most went by road, but some took a shortcut – a boat trip across the Solway – especially if angry parents were hot on their heels. Sadly, some came to grief and drowned."

"Yes, I've heard those stories too, but what about the firework display on the road to Maryport at . . . ?"

"Wolsty Castle."

"Never heard of it before."

"Few have, and I suspect the name Nicolas Flamel means nothing to you either."

"Quite so."

"Wolsty Castle was constructed around 1327 at the request of the Abbot of Holme Cultram Abbey, who wanted a fortified tower as a protection against invading Scottish kings and their armies. In truth the abbey had been trashed in 1216 by Alexander II and then again by Robert the Bruce in 1322. However, for unknown reasons the castle was built five miles from the abbey and consisted of a tower with a gatehouse, curtain wall and small moat. It really wouldn't have been large enough to garrison a defensive force to tackle anything but small raiding parties. Its true function was probably either as a bolthole for the Abbot during such emergencies or even as a place where he would entertain guests.

"Tolerably recently, however, the castle, possibly because of its isolated location in a remote part of the North, has been linked by certain writers of fantasy and folklore with a fourteenth-century French alchemist and necromancer called Nicolas Flamel.

"He is said to have performed his dark arts at Wolsty without fear or hindrance from the abbey. Amongst his many achievements were his control over the sea and the construction of Bolton Old Church or Boltongate All Saints Church in a night. It was even rumoured that he and the Devil between them raised Criffel up from farmland into the imposing hill on the Scottish side of the Solway. Then, finally, despite his satanic connections, Flamel was allowed a Christian burial at Holme Cultram in 1290.

"As it happens, there really was an alchemist of that name. He lived in fourteenth-century Paris, and, on discovering the elixir of life, he is said to have become immortal. This, like the rest, is total fiction as, on his death in 1418, he was laid to rest in a tomb in the nave of St Jacques de la Boucherie."

"So what about the demonic firework display I experienced?" Chibb enquired with increasing frustration. "It seemed real enough at the time."

"Illusions often do, my friend, but someone – whoever it was – must also have known the legend of Nicolas Flamel and his alleged connection with Wolsty Castle . . . and was, for whatever reason, trying to frighten you."

"And that he did!" murmured Chibb under his breath.

"And what of your trip, Yan? Clearly the good Bishop Harvey's ride down the fell and into Bass was an entertaining display and no more. The incident at Castlerigg was something entirely different. Indeed, apart from one major difference, you experienced an almost word-for-word visual display of Wilson Armistead's story 'The Legend of the Druid's Sacrifice'.

"This is an ancient tale from the Iron Age (750 BC to AD 43) of the love of two Carvetii youths, Mudor and Ella, and the compassion of an arch-Druid. It seems that a fever was spreading through the community, killing many, and the verdict of the Druids was that Mogan, one of the gods, had cursed

22

the tribe for its wickedness. Only the sacrificial burning of a virgin would be sufficient to appease him. To Mudor's sorrow, Ella was chosen and duly trussed up in a wicker cage on top of a pyre of wood and dry leaves. The tribe assembled around the ring of stones at Castlerigg – with Druids forming an inner circle. The arch-Druid lit the wood beneath the cage. Then, to the astonishment of all, he raised his arms and implored Mogan to release Ella from this hideous death – which he did, causing water to gush forth from under the fire, thus extinguishing the flames.

"Naturally, this story ends with Mudor and Ella living happily ever after into a ripe old age. It also hints at the ending of the Druidic era and its cruel religion at the hands of the Roman Governor General Gaius Suetonius Paulinus in AD 60, when he invaded the Island of Mona (Anglesey) just prior to the revolt of Queen Boudicca of the Iceni. In fact Armistead's tale is the Victorian equivalent of a medieval morality play."

"I'm not sure that what I saw ended happily," said Yan dejectedly.

"I think you're right there," his father added while giving his son a hug. "And now, Tan, what can we make of your adventure? You didn't see a vampire, but, then again, it seems there probably never was one . . . according to a recent tale Frank has discovered in the college library."

"Yes," Frank said with a smile from ear to ear. "It's an account written by a contemporary of your father – Annony Mouse, the irony monger of Wigton Road – who went on a short holiday with his mother to Croglin in the early 1950s, where two of her cousins lived. He wrote the following: *I was only eight when we went to stay with Tom and Jack Byers*, Frank began.

He was abruptly interrupted by Tan: "I fell asleep with my back against their headstone."

"Yes, and that was the result of too much Newcastle holy water. But, to continue . . . *Uncle Tom and Jack's house was whitewashed inside and out . . . and had no electricity or running water. The fire consisted of dried burning peat blocks and gave the house a pleasant smoky aroma. When we arrived Uncle Jack let us in; his blind brother, Tom, was out on one of his walks.*

"'*He'll come back soaked,' said Uncle Jack. 'He's forever falling into the beck . . . but then he's stone blind!'*

"*Actually, Tom appeared not too much later and was soaked to the skin. While he dried himself in front of the peat fire – his trousers steaming – Mam made our evening meal. She boiled a pan of water containing potatoes and an unopened tin of peas on the fire. They were to be served with cold*

23

tinned corned beef. Unfortunately, the tin's opening mechanism broke and the brothers did not possess a tin opener. Jack did have a heavy-duty gulley knife, which after a few vicious stabs produced a large jagged hole in the tin's top, through which it was possible to spoon out the Fray Bentos meat. It wasn't the best meal I've ever had, but I was very hungry at the time.

"Over a cup of tea – we had also brought a gill of milk with us – the boys began to fill Mam in with what little news they had. Seeing I was totally bored, they began to tell stories to entertain me. One was about the Croglin Vampire, which would not have been totally appropriate for a modern ten-year-old . . . but we were tough in those days, despite the pink-rimmed spectacles I was forced to wear.

"'The story of the so-called Vampire is rubbish.' Uncle Jack declared with relish. 'It was the vicar who was the Vampire! He had a habit of visiting young ladies in their bedrooms after nightfall – to read them fairly stories and the like. On one occasion he was nearly caught and ran off into the graveyard, where, using the gift of the gab – as they say – he managed to persuade everyone that he'd cornered the vampire and dissolved him completely with the aid of a bucket of holy water.

"'When the Bishop found out, the vicar was defrocked and naturally went into politics.' And that, young man, is a true story!"

"Well, I believe him!" Tan said, and he burst out laughing.

"And so did the assizes judge in the county court at Carlisle some years later, when this and other offences were taken into consideration."

"So where do we go from here?" Professor Tethra Hardwick asked the assembled group. "I, for one, am confused. The task Frank Potts and I gave you has raised more questions than answers."

"Well," said Frank, "we knew beforehand that the ghost stories are a load of twaddle, but the fact that so many of those legends are being so vividly reproduced is both alarming and – to say the least – very difficult to explain."

"There is, however, one common denominator in all of those spectacles – the black-robed and hooded figure!" finally added Professor Hardwick.

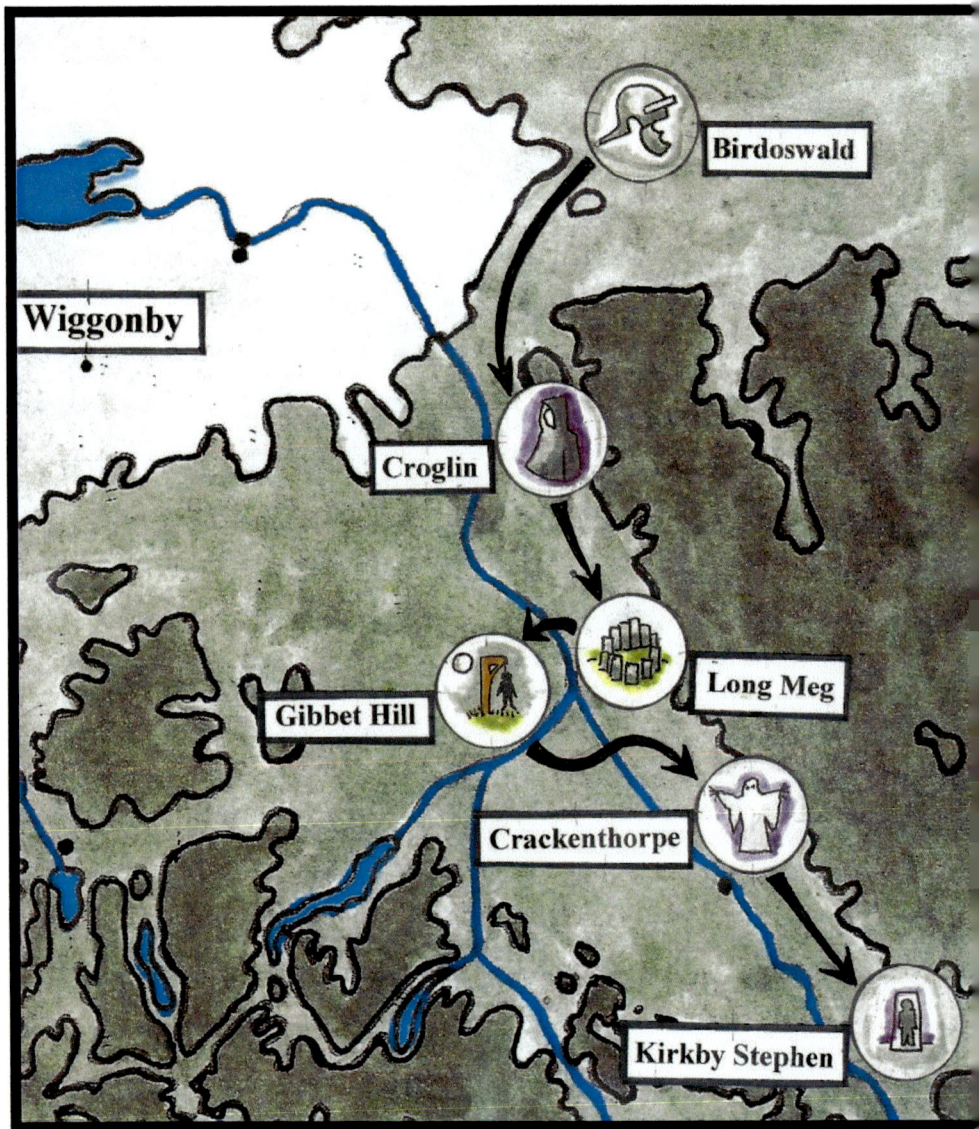

In search of Droopy Drawers.

CHAPTER 4 – THE PLOT THICKENS

By the next morning Wiggonby College's 'fearless ghost-busting vampire-hunters' were down to two. Wolsty Castle had been too much for poor Chibb Swaledale, who, true to form, had locked himself in his 'scriptorium' and refused to come out.

"I'm afraid Frank Potts won't budge from the library either, and I'm too old for such jaunts. So you're on your own for the next mission," Tethra Hardwick confided to his luckless sons.

"What next mission?" Yan and Tan blurted out in unison.

"Why, exploring the east of the county in Hindenburg III!"

"In an airship?"

"No, no, no – it's one of those mini-diddy-weeny what's-it bag o' things. I hired it from a firm in Kirkby Stephen. You'll be away for at least a week and where you're going if there are any hotels – which there aren't – they'll be closed due to the lockdown!"

"Remind me what we're supposed to be up to, please," Tan asked his brother as they headed towards Carlisle in one of Erik Bloodaxe's small but perfectly cosy people carriers. "And who is Erik Bloodaxe when he's at home?"

"As to the latter, he's an entrepreneur, recently moved down from Trondheim, in Norway."

"I suppose he came highly recommended by Ivan the Terrible."

"Apparently not – Ivan's been retired for some time. I'm sure there's nothing to worry about. The company logo is a red axe, and its motto is 'We aim at the public to please', which may have lost something in the translation."

"Doubtless . . . but why are we going to Birdoswald?"

"In the last forty-eight hours there've been a number of sightings of a black-robed and hooded figure between Birdoswald and Kirkby Stephen – probably the same one you met at Croglin. He's apparently quite harmless – unlike the other ones – and he hasn't been terrorising any sheep either. Fatha suggests we should talk to some of the local shepherds, who are all, oddly enough, Philosophy graduates of Wiggonby College."

"Of course. I knew that!" Tan added without conviction.

"Banna was the Roman name for this small fort at Birdoswald on Hadrian's Wall. Like all the other forts, it was manned by auxiliary troops who were originally recruited from all parts of the empire. From AD 122 to 138 the I Tungoram, an infantry unit (*cohors militaria*) from Gallia Belgica, now modern Belgium, manned this fort. After that, it's thought that another infantry unit, the I Aelia Dacorum from Dacia, now modern Romania, served here between AD 222 and 238. Frankly nobody's sure what happened next, but there is some evidence that after the Romans left in the early fifth century a local chieftain and his people occupied Banna and even constructed wooden structures within the fort."

"Thank you, Yan, for the history lesson," Tan remarked after a particularly fine meal, which he had cooked in Hindenburg III's galley.

Yan hadn't time to clip him round the ear as there was a knock at the door. Tan, being the nearest, opened it and, after a brief conversation, returned with a puzzled look on his face.

"There's one of those Irmine Street Roman re-enactors outside, but I can't understand a word he's saying!"

"What did he say?"

"Something like '*Ave, domine. . . . Lac obsecro.*'"

"*Lac obsecro*? Oh, dear! Just give him a glass of milk, smile then bolt the door – he's not a re-enactor!"

The journey south the next morning was totally uneventful, with not a sheep or shepherd in sight for quite some time. Skirting Lanercost Priory then Naworth Castle, they crossed the A69 and took the back roads to Croglin. To Tan's relief they did not tarry in the village, but had to stop a half-mile further south as the road was totally blocked by – as it happened – two large flocks of Herdwicks facing each other menacingly. Behind a drystone wall two men were hacking at each other with long sticks, which turned out to be inverted crooks.

"Good morning." Yan hailed the taller of the two, who had just delivered a coup de grâce to his opponent, who was now lying prone and unconscious on the grass.

"And that'll teach you in future, Elvis Schopenhauer, to treat me, Bing Kirkegaard, with a little more respect!"

"You must be one of my father's philosophy graduates, but why are you thrashing that poor fellow?"

"Actually, we're great friends and we were just sparring – or, as we call it, shaking a stick at each other! It's the inter-flock tachi/katana finals next month and I intend to give Reg Hagel a run for his money."

"Well, best of luck in your philosophical endeavours, and I have to say that I really like your nom de guerre – or is it your real name?"

"No, I changed my name by deed poll! The Professor insisted, before convocation!"

"Good choice – Bing Kirkegaard – but, to change the subject, what can you tell us about the black-robed figure walking about the fells? Our father, your professor, said you might be able to help."

"I think you must mean Droopy Drawers. It's what the sheep – bless them – call him. They don't actually realise we understand every bleat and baa they say. . . . But that's what philosophy is all about, isn't it?"

"That's the clearest definition of philosophy I've heard so far," Yan declared.

Tan, on the other hand, was more direct: "Yes, but why do they call him Droopy Drawers?"

"Well, he sort of mopes about a bit – quite harmless really. He was last seen heading south towards Long Meg."

"It's a little off the beaten track, but we should get there by lunchtime. Do you know about Long Meg?"

"Of course – I've read Rollo and Fatha's book," Tan said with a modicum of frustration. "It's another of those stone-ringy things – between Glassonby and Little Salkeld. It's supposed to be the petrified remains of a witch called Long Meg and her Daughters, who were turned to stone by a magician during one of their covens – doubtless, he was the legendary Nicolas Flamel."

When they arrived another shepherd was grazing his flock in the centre of the 360-foot oval megalithic ring. Smack in the centre, leaning against a menhir – a red sandstone standing stone called Long Meg – was not, as Yan guessed incorrectly, Reg Hagel, but none other than Bob Descartes.

"An understandable and one-time-forgivable mistake," Bob granted Yan while gripping his crook tightly. No, Droopy's not here – try Beacon Hill just outside Penrith, next to the golf course. Don't ask me why – just trust me, I'm a philosopher. You'll need parking for your Hindenburg Mark III, so talk to Bill, the groundsman."

"Looking at the map, there's a tower on a high point to the north-east of Penrith. It's in a wood, but a track leads up from the road opposite the golf course. We can get to it from the Langwathby to Penrith road."

This was exactly what they did, and en route Tan explained why the hill was so called.

"It has nothing to do with the Spanish Armada beacons (which were sited along the Channel coast), but it served as a warning of Scottish raiding war bands and armies from as early as 1296. Other beacons were sited at Carlisle, Kirkoswald and Orton Scar."

"Beacon Hill also had another name: Gibbet Hill," Yan revealed after handing over the driving to Tan. "And, as I recall, it is associated with a grisly tale."

"Not another one!"

"'Fraid so! It all began on market day, Tuesday 18 November 1766, when Thomas Parker, a farmer of Langwathby, after making a bob or two went for a drink or three in the Cross Keys. The landlord wanted him to sleep it off overnight, but Tom insisted that he was perfectly able to walk home. However, at the crossroad of the Beacon and Langwathby roads, near a site called Nancy Dobson's Stone, he was beaten to death by his godson, Thomas Nicholson. The latter was tried and convicted at Carlisle Assizes and duly hanged on 31 August 1767, after which his corpse was hung in chains in an iron cage below the gallows, or gibbet.

"It hung there for months, slowly consumed by maggots. Putrid pieces of his body fell to the ground, where they were fought over by foxes and feral dogs. Finally, during a wild storm in March 1768, the gibbet fell down . . . after which what remained of Tom Nicholson's bones were buried in an unmarked grave in unhallowed ground.

"The story doesn't end there, as in 1775 a five-year-old boy, accompanied by a servant, was riding along the track where the gallows had once stood. In its stead were three initials, 'T.P.M.', carved on a stone, which, as the servant explained in vivid detail to the boy, meant 'Thomas Parker's Murderer was hanged here.' Doubtless the resultant nightmares spawned a poem which the boy, William Wordsworth, now aged twenty-nine, wrote in 1799.

"A relevant passage goes as follows:

> "Dismounting, down the rough and stony moor
> I led my horse, and, stumbling on, at length
> Came to a bottom, where in former times
> A murderer had been hung in iron chains.
> The gibbet-mast had mouldered down, the bones
> And iron case were gone; but on the turf,
> Hard by, soon after the fell deed was wrought
> Some unknown hand had carved the murderer's name."

"Sounds as if William had mixed up the names," Tan declared to Yan astonishment, who'd been paying attention for once.

"Well, that's called poetic licence, I suppose. Now, let's look for Bill the groundsman and then look for this tower marked on the map."

It was late afternoon and dark clouds were lowering menacingly above them as they climbed up the steep rough stony track. By the time they reached the top, the light had all but faded away and in the clearing instead of a red sandstone two-storey tower . . . was a gibbet and metal cage, the latter swinging eerily and sounding like chalk on a blackboard. The corpse within turned its head, revealing eyes like glowing coals.

At that precise instant, from behind them came a sound like someone clicking his fingers. Startled, they turned round and saw a black-robed and hooded figure.

As it and the gibbet melted away into the gloom, a clear voice uttered five words: "The Cathedral in the Dales."

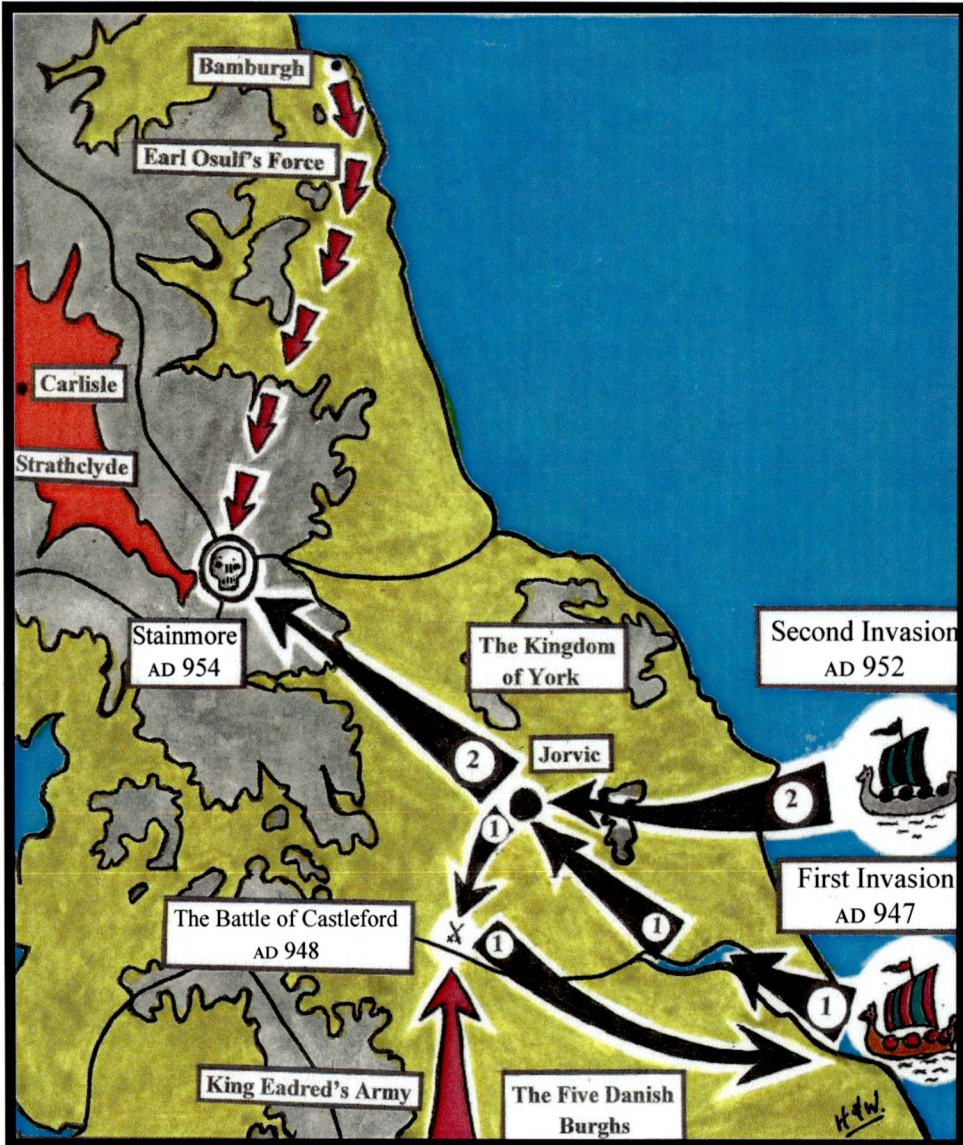

Bamburgh

Earl Osulf's Force

Carlisle

Strathclyde

Stainmore
AD 954

The Kingdom
of York

Second Invasion
AD 952

Jorvic

2

1

The Battle of Castleford
AD 948

First Invasion
AD 947

1

King Eadred's Army

The Five Danish
Burghs

The campaigns of Erik Bloodaxe as King of Jorvic/York (AD 947 to 954), the first ending with his defeat by King Eadred at the Battle of Castleford and the second with his murder by Earl Osulf of Bamburgh at the behest of King Eadred on Stainmore.

CHAPTER 5 – SHOULD AULD ACQUAINTANCE BE FORGOT

"The Cathedral in the Dales?"

"Well, Tan, I thought you'd never ask. It's to the south, in a village we have been heading to all along. It's also known as Kirkby Stephen's St John's Parish Church."

"That's where we have to return Hindenburg III to Mr Bloodaxe, isn't it?"

"No, I think not, Tan. The late Erik Bloodaxe – the former King of Norway and Jorvik – was killed at the Battle of Stainmore in the Pennines in AD 954 at the hands of Osulf, Earl of Bamburgh – not that far from Kirkby Stephen, as it happens, which is probably why Droopy Drawers called the car-hire company by that name."

"Droopy Drawers?"

"Yes, he's the one who's been leading us by the nose for some time."

The journey south was pleasant enough. Just north of Appleby, Yan, who was navigating, pointed out the village of Crackenthorpe on the left.

"Now, almost immediately on the right, overlooking the Eden is Crackenthorpe Hall, which was the ancestral home of the Machell family. They are supposed to have lived hereabouts for well over 1,000 years.

"The hall was haunted by the wife of Lancelot Machell, Peg Sleddall, but isn't now – the family saw to that. As the story goes, after her death in the middle to late seventeenth century, the 'Grey Lady' would appear from time to time riding at breakneck speed through the village and grounds of the estate in a coach pulled by horses – usually when the 'helm wind' blew down from the Pennines."

"Which was?"

"A cold, howling breeze, arising from helmet-shaped clouds topping the fells."

"A good day to stay indoors, then?"

"Doubly so for the Machells, as Peg's appearance foretold a death in the family. Well, after a few of the 'ten little Indians' had popped their clogs, the rest decided to act. They dug her up and reburied her under a large granite block in the Eden just below the hall, which they named Peg's Stone.

"Still there?"

"Not sure, but the Machells weren't the only aristocratic family in the country with a relative who refused to rest in peace."

"Good Lord!"

"Yes, the story goes that one of the Lowthers – Jemmy to his friends and Bad Lord Lowther to the peasants – was a coarse fellow and a spendthrift. He even owed money to Wordsworth's father. Well, nobody lives forever, but Jemmy wasn't going to take death lying down. At his own funeral he apparently attacked the vicar."

"I really would have liked to see that!"

"Well, Tan, Jemmy became quite a nuisance, causing havoc here, there and everywhere – almost making Lowther Castle uninhabitable."

"So the family got out the spades."

"Yes, but I suspect the actual digging was performed by estate workers."

"And where did they finally plant him?"

"In Haweswater under a massive rock called the Stone of Wallow Crag – the very rock which had fallen into the lake as William Charles, the Poet of Kentmere Vale, was born.

"Riveting! But did the stone put an end to the haunting?"

"Apparently it did."

They arrived at Kirkby Stephen around noon and parked in the market square, which was a short walk from the church. On entry Yan bought a small brochure and placed a pound coin in the honesty box. After a short perusal of his purchase, he promptly dragged Tan into the South or Hartley/Musgrave Chapel near the main altar.

"Look around you, Tan – this is history. For instance, that stone coffin lid once covered the only remains of Sir Andrew de Harcla, who was created Earl of Carlisle in 1322 for his defence of the city against Robert the Bruce. Sadly, after his death Sarah, his sister, could only find a few bones to put in his tomb."

"The undertaker was a bit rough or clumsy, I take it,." Tan said rather offhandedly.

"No, of course not. That apology for a king, Edward II, who got his

34

comeuppance at Berkeley Castle at the end of a red-hot poker, accused him of treason in 1323, which resulted in Sir Andrew being hanged, drawn and quartered on Gallows Hill to the south of Carlisle. The tarred head was put on a spike on the Rickergate – the west gate of the city. Where the four quarters were dispatched to is not known. De Harcla was never pardoned and after years of searching only the leg bones were found.

"His story doesn't quite end there. In 1847, for reasons which are not entirely clear, that tomb over there – of Sir Richard Musgrave (1398–1464) – was opened and in it were found not only the remains of Sir Richard, but also a wild boar's tusk and the leg bones of Sir Andrew de Harcla!"

"Well I never!" Tan declared.

"The boar – apparently the last one killed in Westmorland – was a victim of Sir Richard Musgrave's lance, and presumably Sir Andrew's tomb was so damaged at the time that his bones were moved in with Sir Richard's."

"Fascinating!"

"There is another connection between the de Harclas and the Musgraves. After Sir Andrew de Harcla's execution Hartley Castle was given by Edward II to Ralph Neville, 1st Baron Neville of Raby, who in due course sold it to Sir Thomas Musgrave, the 1st Lord Musgrave – the great-great-grandfather of Sir Richard Musgrave, who was a retainer of Richard Neville, the Kingmaker."

"I'm really glad you confided in me about all that," Tan said with total insincerity, "but I'm now going outside to get some fresh air and bang my head on some railings."

With that he turned and headed for the south porch, but just before exiting the church stopped in his tracks and shouted for his brother to come and look at a three-foot-tall carved block of red sandstone. It was an eighth-century carving of Loki, the Norse god of mischief, disguise and mayhem.

"Remind you of anything?" Tan enquired.

"Yes."

"The cross at St Mary's at Gosforth in West Cumberland."

"Definitely!"

Just then from behind them came another voice from a hooded figure dressed in a long black robe: "But you have to admit this one is not very flattering."

Startled, Yan and Tan turned round and involuntarily blurted out, "Droopy Drawers?"

"Not really," said the figure, casting aside his canon's habit, revealing beneath a black suit of which the only redeeming feature was a white clerical collar.

"The Reverend Gunnar Mangison?"

"I was once . . . but what's in a name? And, in any case, the difference between fact and fiction is often the thickness of a page in a book!"

"You sound like one of my father's shepherd philosophers," Yan declared.

"Well, I've been that too. What was my name then? Ah, yes – Bing Kirkegaard, as I recall. A bit of a giveaway really, don't you agree? Well, that's enough of this banter. Let's get down to why we're all here before the real vicar turns up. Firstly, the Herdwick War is now well and truly over – along with all the other spectral apparitions and eye-catching illusions. They were just sprats to catch two mackerel."

"I presume you're referring to us?" Yan interjected.

"Quite so, and the reason for all this subterfuge and the trail of stone breadcrumbs was to see if you were both up to the task in hand, which I am about to dangle before you. Truly, it's a challenge well worth your consideration, and one which the historians haven't been able to solve."

"Interesting," replied Tan, "but what is it?"

"You must agree to undertake the quest first."

Yan looked and Tan and they both nodded to each other.

"Agreed," they said in unison.

"It's quite simple: all you have to do is to find out what happened to the real Droopy Drawers between May 1464 and July 1465."

"The real Droopy Drawers?"

"Yes – Henry Plantagenet, otherwise known as King Henry VI of England. After the Battle of Hexham on Sunday 15 May 1464 he disappeared and is said to have wandered alone, criss-crossing the Lake District for over a year. He was finally betrayed and handed over to the Yorkist forces of King Edward IV near Clitheroe in Northern Lancashire on Thursday 13 July 1465."

Sir Andrew de Harcla.

The Loki Stone.

Droopy Drawers.

39

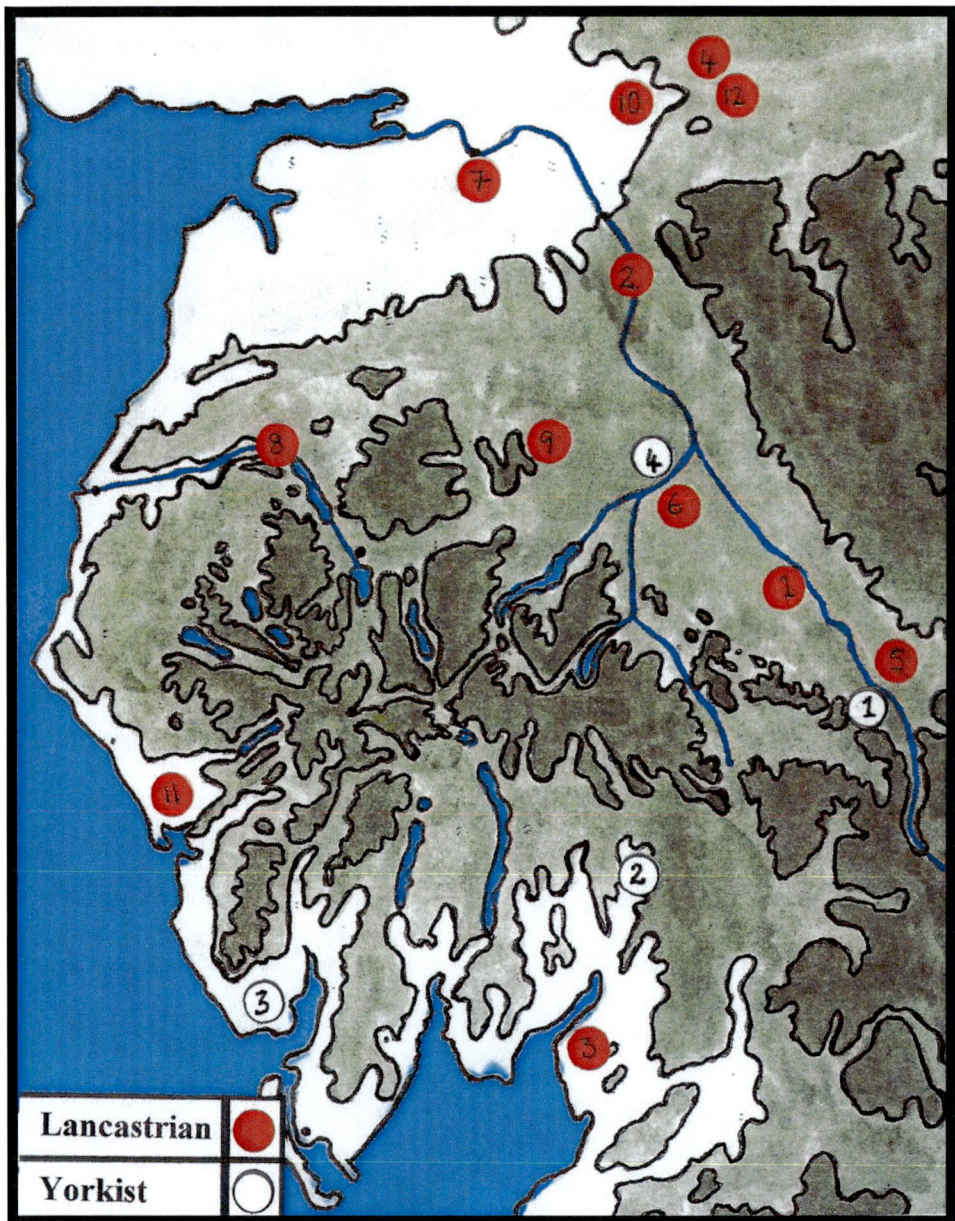

Cumbrian castles – pre-Towton (1461).

CHAPTER 6 – *QUO VADIMUS?*

"Let me see," Tethra Hardwick pondered. "If I understand correctly, what you are trying to tell me is that you finally caught up with the black-robed and hooded figure in the Parish Church of St John's at Kirkby Stephen with the aid of one of my philosopher shepherds, Bing Kirkegaard."

"Correct!" the boys replied.

"Bing referred to the creature as Droopy Drawers, who you also believe was both Blokey Bill of Blackpool and the Reverend Gunnar Mangison of Gosforth, Cumbria."

"Also correct, and he may also have been your Erik Bloodaxe."

"I never met him – the contract for Hindenburg III was made over the telephone! And are you also saying that Bing was also, like all the rest, Loki, the Norse god of mischief and disguise?"

"I couldn't have put it better," said Tan.

"Well, whatever tablets you're both taking, I should double the dose immediately!"

All three looked at each other and, almost telepathically, it was agreed that a tea break was called for.

Chibb Swaledale duly delivered the Earl Grey and Chocolate Hobnob biscuits, after which, with measured words, Tethra said, "You have both involved yourselves in a TMHTSO problem, which is an abbreviation for an in-phrase amongst historians and archaeologists. It means 'too much hassle to sort out', which is why they never tried to decipher the medieval carvings in Carlisle Castle – lazy beggars!"

"Fatha, you worked out the connection between Halfdan Ragnarsson's invasion and St Cuthbert's seventeen-year 1,200-mile journey in his coffin, so why shouldn't we try to discover what happened to Henry VI?" Yan asked.

"St Cuthbert's journey is an historical fact, but this borders on legend and all legends should have been left in the beer mugs from which they sprang! If you two really want to try to solve a conundrum set by someone who might well be an historian, skilled in illusions – someone who is trying to find halfwits to do the donkeywork prior to publishing his next book – then who am I to stop you?"

Undaunted by their father's opposition to their becoming involved in the Henry VI project, both boys began the seemingly unending task of reading book after book of musty-smelling volumes which Frank Potts kept piling up in front of them. It wasn't long before exasperation set in – striking Tan first.

"Well, Yan, it's no wonder the historians wouldn't tackle this problem. It's impossible! So where do we go from here?"

Yan looked up from a particularly boring tome and declared with equal vigour, "We have so little to go on – a beginning in Bywell Castle near Hexham and an end at Brungerley Bridge near Clitheroe. In between we have one visit to Muncaster Castle and possibly two to Crackenthorpe Hall, near Appleby. Other than that we have very little to go on – these books aren't in the least bit helpful."

Tan agreed and then, pushing aside his pile of books, laid on the table four maps.

"The first two are new. Frank has sweated blood to produce them. They show the castles in Cumbria and which force – whether Lancastrian or Yorkist – was in command of them. The first is dated just before the Battle of Towton on 29 March 1461, and the other covers the period of Henry VI's journey, between mid-1464 and mid-1465. The other two you've seen before. They show the monasteries in Cumbria and the Roman roads and forts in the county."

"I think, Yan, this is the point from which we should start our investigation – where could he have gone and how could he possibly have evaded capture?"

Yan photocopied a set of the four maps for himself and then added, "Actually, we need to know an awful lot of background history – not just of England, but also of France and Burgundy. There's also the matter of Henry VI's health – leave that to me."

A few days later they met again to discuss the progress they'd both made. Tan laid on the table a few 'blank' maps, which he'd prepared with Frank's help. They covered Northern England from Bamburgh in Northumberland to as far south as Clitheroe in Lancashire. They would serve to plot stages or phases in Henry's journey.

Yan looked pleased – just like the cat who'd found the cream.

"Actually, I think I've discovered something which has been overlooked, but I'm not entirely sure at the moment."

"At least give me a clue, brother."

"In a word, genetics."

Tan yawned.

"I also think my theory answers why France became involved in the Armagnac/Burgundian Civil War and the English not only perpetuated the Hundred Years War, but also became entangled in the Wars of the Roses.

"What I am about to tell you spans nearly three-quarters of a century, starting around 1392 – that is according to the thirteen autobiographical *Commentaries* of Pope Pius II, which, although written around 1460, were not actually published until 1585, and then posthumously by a relative called Cardinal Francesco Bandini Piccolomini.

"The story begins with the delusions and strange behaviour of Charles VI, King of France, who thought he was made of glass and insisted that iron bars should be sewn into his clothes, lest being touched by anyone he shattered into pieces.

"He was a fearful person and quite obviously mentally unstable. In fact, it's thought he was a paranoid schizophrenic. There is also a suggestion that he had inherited this illness from his mother, Joanna of Bourbon, the wife of Charles V. She had suffered a psychotic illness in 1372 after the birth of the second of her three children, Louis of Orleans. This illness seems to have been a severe episode of postnatal depression and as such not genetic – there was no recurrence after the birth of her next child or, indeed, in the remaining six years of her life.

"Charles VI, as a medieval king, had not only to be politically strong to control domestic issues, but also had to be endowed with both diplomatic and military skills to combat troublesome neighbouring countries. If a monarch hadn't these qualities or was unable to rule his lands for a significant length of time, then measures would ultimately be taken to replace him. The question of insanity as a reason for a king's incompetence had not arisen previously in France, but it certainly did in 1392.

"Two opposing factions emerged – not to replace Charles VI, but to vie for control of the Regency Council, which was directing the affairs of France during his recurring bouts of insanity.

"Initially, his wife, Isabella of Bavaria, acted solely as regent, but she was soon joined by Charles's uncle, John Valois 'the Bold', Duke of

Burgundy and leader of the Burgundian faction.

"Not long afterwards, Charles VI's brother, John, Duke of Orleans, became not only Isabella's chief advisor, but also her lover. In addition he assumed the leadership of the Orleans Party, which became known as the Armagnac Faction when Bernard VII, Count of Armagnac, assumed control.

"In 1404 John the Fearless became Duke of Burgundy. He was a man of action. Discontented both with his diminishing importance and because he had lost Luxemburg to Louis of Orleans, he struck. Louis was assassinated in Paris on 23 November 1407, and this resulted in his son, Charles of Orleans, preparing for war. The low-grade civil war which ensued rumbled on for years without either side gaining the upper hand for long.

Meanwhile in 1415 Henry V of England took advantage of the chaos in France and sailed to Normandy with an army. John the Fearless of Burgundy developed a bout of diplomatic flu and was neutral during Henry V's successful campaign, which ended in a resounding victory over the French at the Battle of Agincourt on 25 October 1415.

"The French civil war continued to smoulder on until, one fateful day, the Dauphin of France, Charles Valois – actually the fifth son and fifth Dauphin during the reign of Charles VI – invited John the Fearless to discuss peace proposals. This meeting was to have occurred – under strict rules of guaranteed protection for all parties – on 10 September 1419 at Montereau, some forty miles south-east of Paris. John's acceptance turned out to be a very bad idea indeed. Charles, recalling the brutal assassination of his Uncle Louis in Paris in 1407, undoubtedly on the instigation of John the Fearless, duly arranged for the Duke of Burgundy to be hacked to death on the bridge at Montereau.

"The next Duke of Burgundy, Philip the Good, lost no time in arranging an alliance with Henry V, which resulted in the Treaty of Troyes on 21 May 1420. The co-signatories of the treaty were Henry V of England, Philip the Good of Burgundy and Isabella of Bavaria, wife of Charles VI.

"At the heart of the treaty was a simple proclamation that, on the death of Charles VI, Henry V or his heir would be crowned King of France – to the exclusion of the Dauphin, Charles Valois.

"Another condition of the agreement was that Henry V should marry Charles VI's daughter, Catherine of Valois. This he duly did on 2 June that year, in Troyes, either in the Cathedral of St Pierre et St Paul or in the Parish Church of St Jean-au-Marche.

"Sadly, Henry V died on 31 August 1422 of dysentery in Vincennes while on campaign, two months before the demise of Charles VI on 21 October. Henry V was never crowned King of France. He did, however, leave behind an heir – his nine-month-old son, Henry Plantagenet.

"History, as it often does, was about to repeat itself. Both Charles VI and Henry VI were minors when their fathers died – Charles was eleven and Henry was only nine months old. Neither being old enough to reign, they both grew up under regencies, headed by their uncles.

"Charles VI was crowned King of France at the age of eleven on 4 November 1380 at Reims Cathedral, whereas Henry VI achieved the unique and dual privilege of being crowned King of England, aged eight, at Westminster Abbey on 6 November 1429 and then, aged ten, King of France in Paris in Notre Dame on 16 December 1431.

"Neither boys assumed their full regal powers until later. In Charles VI's case it was in 1389, when he was aged twenty-one; as for Henry VI, he was sixteen years of age and the year was 1437.

"Their marriages are dated as follows – Charles VI was aged seventeen when he married the fifteen-year-old Isabella of Bavaria in 1385, whereas twenty-three-year-old Henry VI married the fifteen-year-old Margaret of Anjou, a niece of Charles VII, in 1445.

"Very little is known about Charles VI as he grew up; but much more is known about Henry VI. Henry was apparently shy and pious, but not particularly bright or scholastic. He wasn't at all militarily inclined and was averse to bloodshed. He was probably quite naïve and certainly hated deception. All in all, he had few qualities befitting a medieval king.

"As he grew older, things didn't improve much. His marriage didn't start off too well as Henry needed tuition in the bedroom department – a skill which he may not have perfected, as it wasn't long before his teenage wife was alleged to have taken a lover, Edmund Beaufort, 2nd Duke of Somerset. Court rumours persisted, and some even implied that Henry VI was not the father of Edward, Prince of Wales, whom he regarded as a 'miracle'. This would have been compatible with his lifelong aversion to human physical contact.

"Henry's first and most serious mental breakdown occurred in 1453, when was aged thirty-one – a little older than Charles VI's at twenty-four years. Poor Henry was ill for at least twelve months, during which time he was apparently totally unresponsive. It is said that he was not even aware of his baby son when the child was placed in his lap. This sounds very much like catatonic schizophrenia, which he may have inherited from his grandfather, Charles VI of France.

"It wasn't long, despite Queen Margaret and Edmund Beaufort's attempts to conceal the news, before the true state of the King's health leaked out. He did recover – to a degree – but he obviously was even less able to govern than previously.

"And here's another coincidence, Tan. As in Charles VI's illness, the English court was riven by discontent due to a long list of grievances. The Hundred Years War had ended badly, with England retaining only a small fraction of her French possessions. These were further diminished by the Treaty of Tours of March 1444, the disastrous wedding settlement urged on Henry VI by Cardinal Beaufort and William de la Pole, 1st Duke of Suffolk. The actual terms, which were supposed to end the Hundred Years War amicably, were virtually dictated to Suffolk from a distance by Charles VII, who hadn't forgotten the Treaty of Troyes, by which the English had attempted to exclude him from ever being crowned King of France.

"In a nutshell, there would be no dowry from Renee, Duke of Anjou and Margaret's father, and the truce would only last twenty-one months – hardly a final solution to such a long conflict. The worst part of the deal was that Maine and Anjou would be handed over to Charles VII – parts of France which had been in English hands for over 300 years, since the days when Matilda, daughter of Henry I and wife of Geoffrey of Anjou, had fought Stephen of Blois for the English throne.

"Suffolk suspected the loss of Maine and Anjou would be an anathema to his countrymen. He was tried and convicted of treason, but his friend Henry VI reduced the sentence to banishment. He didn't get very far from the English coast, as off Dover on 2 May 1450 his ship was intercepted by the *Nicholas of the Tower*. He was subjected to a much less formal trial, found guilty and then put into a rowing boat, where a sailor sawed off his head – with a rusty hacksaw, if an oft-told story can be believed.

"Meanwhile, onshore, two separate factions which had been growing in strength for many months began preparing in earnest for the coming conflict. Men were being recruited and trained for a civil war which would last for forty-two years.

"On one side were the Lancastrians, the King's faction, later depicted in Tudor times as the bearers of a red-rose emblem. They were led by Edmund Beaufort, 2nd Duke of Somerset. Opposing them were the Yorkists – bearers of a white-rose emblem – led by Richard Plantagenet, 3rd Duke of York, who was the leading English magnate at that time. His regal credentials were impeccable, being both a great-grandson of Edward III on his father's side and a great-great-great-grandson of the same king on his mother's side.

"Apart from the aforesaid grievances, the Yorkist faction had two other 'stones in their shoes' – firstly, there was the mishandling of the country's governance by royal advisors like Edmund Beaufort (2nd Duke of Beaufort); and secondly, there was Henry VI's interfering French wife, Margaret of Anjou – the She-Wolf of France – who rubbed everyone up the wrong way, except, of course, Edmund Beaufort.

"The first battle of the Wars of the Roses, or Wars of the Cousins, was fought at St Albans on 22 May 1455. This was really a surprise attack (rather than a formal battle) by Richard, Duke of York, on the King and his armed retinue, which was heading up to Leicester for a Grand Council meeting. Richard's intention was not to kill Henry VI, but to capture him and in so doing to set in motion a mechanism by which he, Richard Plantagenet, would succeed to the throne after Henry's natural death – shades of Henry V and King Charles VI in the Treaty of Troyes in 1422. However, just like those of Henry V, the aspirations of Richard Duke of York would never come to fruition.

"The most prominent casualty at the first Battle of St Albans was Edmund Beaufort, 2nd Duke of Somerset, with whom Richard of York had had a long-standing and bitter quarrel. Edmund was probably searched for by a picked group of Richard's retainers, and butchered as he tried to escape from the Castle Inn, where he had sought refuge. This set in motion a murderous precedent of score-settling after battles, which would backfire on Richard and his son, Edmund, Duke of Rutland, after the Battle of Wakefield on 30 December 1460.

"Henry played no part in his first battle, which lasted only half an hour, and he was captured near the end of the fighting – an unfortunate habit, which he would repeat more than once. He was similarly apprehended in his tent by a Yorkist archer called Henry Mountford at the Battle of Northampton on 10 July 1460. His third and final capture – or, rather, rescue on this occasion by Lancastrians – occurred during the Second Battle of St Albans on 17 February 1461, when he was discovered sitting under a tree singing psalms while the conflict ranged round him.

"Judged to be a complete liability, this would be the last time he would be allowed anywhere near a battlefield and why he was safely tucked away in Bywell Castle while the Battle of Hexham was being lost by his forces on 15 May 1464.

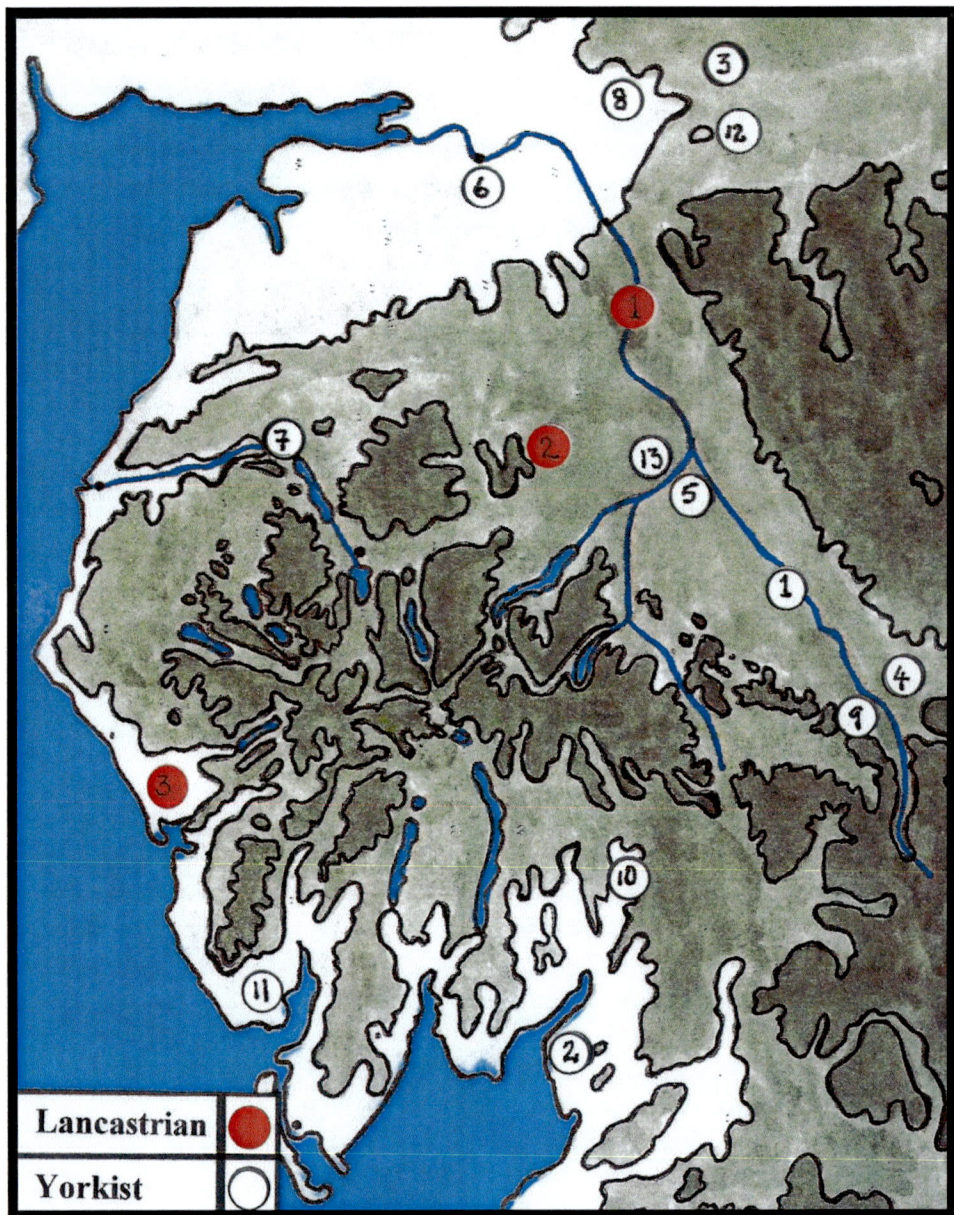

Cumbrian castles (1464–1465).

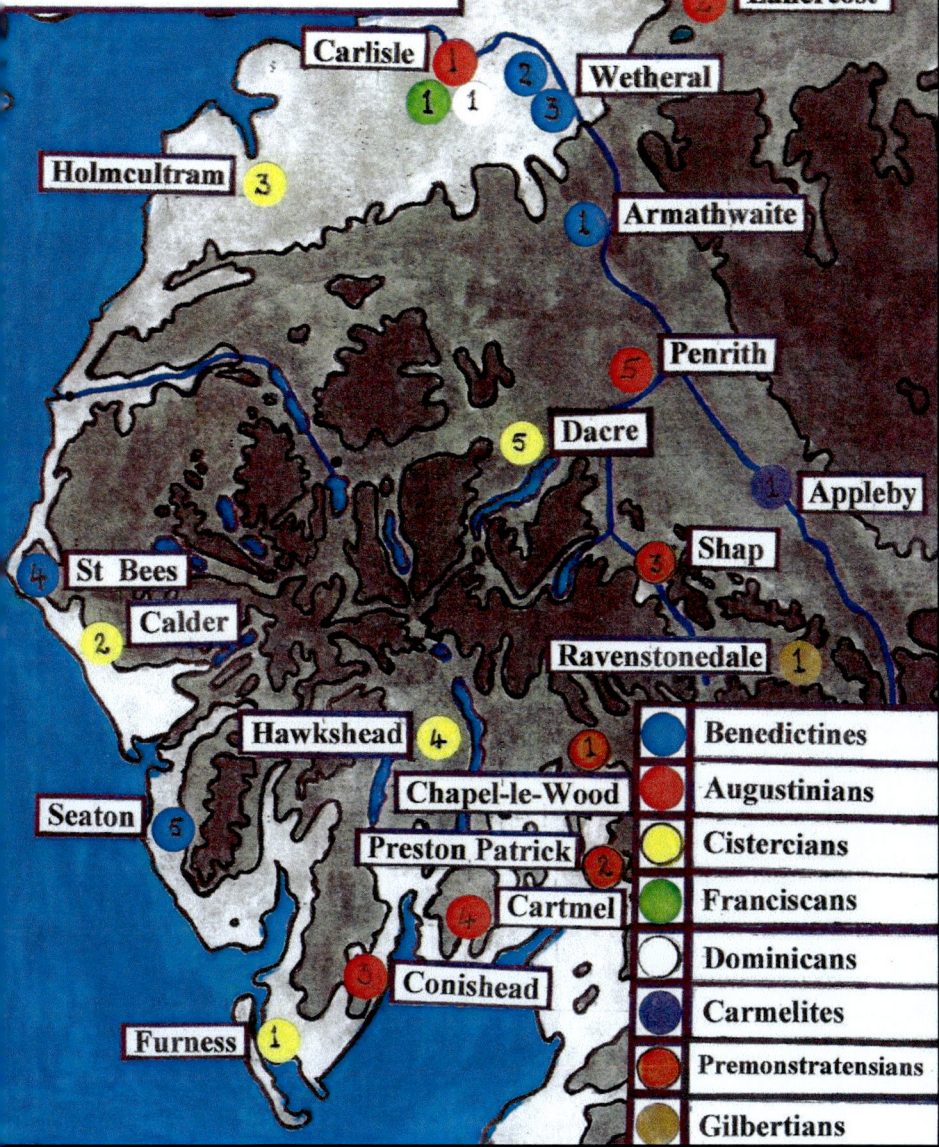

Monasteries in Cumbria
(AD 1089–1540)

Lanercost

Carlisle

Wetheral

Holmcultram

Armathwaite

Penrith

Dacre

Appleby

St Bees

Shap

Calder

Ravenstonedale

Hawkshead

Chapel-le-Wood

Seaton

Preston Patrick

Cartmel

Conishead

Furness

🔵	Benedictines
🔴	Augustinians
🟡	Cistercians
🟢	Franciscans
⚪	Dominicans
🔵	Carmelites
🔴	Premonstratensians
🟤	Gilbertians

King Henry VI of England.

CHAPTER 7 – THE ROAD TO HEXHAM

"You know, Yan, I think you're right. Henry VI did inherit his mental illness from his grandfather, Charles VI of France, and the resultant political mismanagement by inept regencies and adulterous queens in France and then England resulted in the development of irreconcilable factions in both countries, which in turn caused an unstoppable descent into the respective French and English civil wars.

"Equally, it is unquestionable that the political fate of England mirrored that of France, because the same conditions steered both countries to disaster – and all because of a genetically determined mental illness in an underage heir, whose father had died too young."

"Thank you, Tan. I think we are now in a better position to understand how Henry VI found himself in such precarious position, before he began his journey in that fateful summer of 1464 – but we are not quite there. We need to know how he was propelled along that road to Hexham.

"Thankfully it isn't necessary to follow his every step from the very onset of the conflict, which began with the First Battle of St Albans on 22 May 1455, but we do need to understand what happened in the early months of 1461.

"Shortly after the Second Battle of St Albans, on 17 February 1461, when Henry VI had been released from the clutches of Richard Neville, Earl of Warwick, the reunited Lancastrian royal family along with its victorious army headed back to York to regroup.

"As they did so, the gates of London were opened to both Warwick and the new leader of the Yorkists, Edward, Earl of March, the eldest son of Richard, 3rd Duke of York, who had been brutally executed along with his seventeen-year-old son, Edmund, Earl of Rutland, after the Battle of Wakefield on 30 December 1460. The Earl of March was duly proclaimed King Edward IV by Warwick on 4 March, but there was no time to celebrate or tarry – hence the combined forces of Edward and

Warwick also headed north in close pursuit of their quarry.

"The two forces met at Towton on Palm Sunday, 29 March 1461, just eight miles south-west of York, and fought in a blinding snowstorm. The Lancastrians lost badly and the butcher's bill for them was an estimated 9,000 dead, as opposed to around 1,000 on the Yorkist side. Defeat was followed by a headlong rout.

"News of the disaster was swiftly carried to Margaret of Anjou, Henry VI and young Prince Edward in York, who then, along with the Lancastrian army commanders Somerset (Edmund Beaufort), Exeter and Roos, subsequently fled northward to Scotland, where they were greeted warmly by the Queen Mother, Mary of Guelders, and her nine-year-old son, King James III.

"Negotiations between the two queens resulted in men and materiel reinforcing the remnants of the Lancastrian force, but it wasn't quite enough to make a difference. Somerset and then Hungerford were sent to France to beg for aid, but without success. Then, in the spring of 1462, a desperate Margaret of Anjou personally went to France to negotiate with the new king, Louis XI, her cousin. Again the support given was insufficient. On her return to Scotland the war raged on. The castles of Alnwick, Bamburgh, Dunstanburgh and Northam changed hands time and time again, but no decisive or permanent impact could be made against the Yorkist war machine.

"Finally, in late July 1463 Margaret and her son sailed for Sluys in the hope of persuading Philip the good, Duke of Burgundy, to give her troops, ships, war materiel and money – but she was out of luck. He packed her off to her father, Renee of Anjou, who kept her a virtual prisoner in the Chateau of St Michel de Barrois for the next seven years.

"Meanwhile, in November, 1463, Henry VI was still in Edinburgh, waiting for his wife to return with a Burgundian army. It was at this point that James Kennedy, Bishop of St Andrews and former Chancellor of Scotland, took pity on Henry. Actually, the Bishop was fulfilling a promise he had given years previously to the French King, Charles VII, to look after Henry, his hapless nephew, if the poor soul needed help – which, as it happened, at that precise moment he did.

"Peace negotiations between the representatives of Edward IV of England and Mary of Guelders were well under way and a serious risk was looming that Henry might soon be extradited back to England. James Kennedy initially whisked Henry off to St Andrews, and then in early December he secretly had his charge transported over the Border to Bamburgh Castle, which was once more back in Lancastrian hands.

"To Henry's misfortune, and within days of his arriving at Bamburgh, Henry Beaufort, 3rd Duke of Somerset, turned up at the castle gates on 8

December 1463 – almost a year after he had surrendered that same castle to Richard Neville, Earl of Warwick, on 26 December 1462.

"Somerset (although goodness knows why) along with Sir Ralph Percy had been pardoned by Edward IV on 10 May 1463, but the ungrateful Duke, bored no doubt by inactivity and his semi-detention in Holt Castle, North Wales, broke bail and escaped. The fortunes of the Lancastrian cause were at a very low ebb and weren't about to be improved by Henry Beaufort, who should have been sent packing by Henry VI had he been in a fit state of mind to do so – which clearly he still wasn't.

"Henry Beaufort, on receiving information that Warwick's younger brother, John Neville, Lord Montagu, was heading north to the Scottish border with instructions to pick up and then escort James III's envoys south to York, decided to launch a surprise attack. It failed miserably and Beaufort's force was trounced on 25 April at a place called Hedgeley Moor.

"Somerset scuttled back to Bamburgh and, having demonstrated his tactical ineptitude against a much better soldier, then decided to reveal his total lack of strategic military skill. And, as it turned out, he did so against the same much more competent commander. With a force of only a few thousand – plus Henry VI – Somerset headed up the Tyne Valley towards Hexham with the hopeful intention of raising a large force with which to later take on the Yorkist army, which he felt would soon be heading north to capture Bamburgh and Henry VI.

"He can't have expected Lord Montagu, who had returned to his base in Newcastle, to follow and engage his forces near Hexham – which is exactly what happened on 15 May. Unfortunately, Montagu arrived with a much larger force, which promptly defeated Somerset, whose army was poorly positioned and unprepared.

"Somerset was promptly beheaded there and then, along with Lord Roos. Robert, 3rd Baron Hungerford, received the same fate later that day in Newcastle. Sir William Tailboys, on the other hand, escaped from the battlefield, but was discovered down a coal mine near Newcastle with the entire funds of the Lancastrian army – some 3,000 marks. He lost his head on 26 May, also in Newcastle."

"But, Yan, what happened to Henry VI? I'm all ears."

"Well, just about the only thing that Henry Beaufort did correctly in May 1464 was to leave his king in Bywell Castle – six and a half miles to the east of Hexham – on the north bank of the River Tyne. Beaufort had remembered not to take him to the battlefield . . . and that, Tan, is where King Henry VI's magical mystery tour began and where we must travel to in the morning to start our journey of detection and discovery."

Bywell Castle.

CHAPTER 8 – FROM LITTLE ACORNS . . .
(Phase 1)

"And that is Bywell Castle?" Yan said, leaning against Hindenburg III.

"Apparently so."

"All I can see is a three-storey grey square crenellated tower with four corner turrets, the remains of a curtain wall and a large arched doorway."

"Well, that's what it looks like on Google Earth too, but it must have been bigger when the Nevilles built it in 1430 . . . I guess."

At that precise moment a stray Durham police patrol car pulled up behind their people carrier and out climbed two patrolmen. One sat on the bonnet and began to juggle three tasers with his left hand, and twirled what looked to be a black baseball bat with his right.

"Impressive," said Tan as the other policeman drew near.

"Out for a joyride, boys?" he said with conviction written all over his face.

"Not really."

"Testing your eyesight?"

"No."

"Looking for that well-known beauty spot Barnie – otherwise known as Barnard Castle?"

"No."

"Is either one of you called Dominic?"

"No. I'm Tan Hardwick and he's my brother Yan. We're out on an historical survey on behalf of the Prince of Wales and the late King Henry VI. I would like to show you our royal credentials, but then I'd have to kill myself."

"So everything's in order, then?"

"Absolutely, officer."

"You sure your name isn't Dominic?"

"Really, do I look like a dipstick?"

"No, you look like a Philosopher-Shepherd."

And with that the boys in blue left.

"Well, what do we really know about what happened here?" Tan asked, thinking it was about time they got down to business.

"Henry VI was brought here before the Battle of Hexham and left almost immediately his army was routed. He left behind his crown, his sword and helmet . . . and some horse trappings."

"Left in a hurry – but with whom?"

"I suspect with the person who had been guarding him ever since he left Bamburgh."

"Any ideas?"

"Well, Sir Humphrey Neville, one of the Westmorland Nevilles, is known to have been at Hexham, but not in the actual battle. Shortly afterwards, he returned to Bamburgh and became second in command to Sir Ralph Grey. As far as I'm concerned, he's our man," Yan said with confidence.

"Do you think he asked the king what they should do next?" Tan said without thinking.

"No way! After only a couple of days in Henry's company, I've no doubt he wouldn't have enquired of him if it was raining. I think as soon as he heard the battle was lost he quickly surmised that the most sensible thing to do was to take Henry back to Bamburgh."

"To Bamburgh?"

"He couldn't just wait for Montagu to arrive. That would have been risky for himself and failing in his duty to Henry VI. Escaping and leaving Henry to his fate would have been equally dishonourable.

"If, on the other hand, they both rode west, it would have been smack into the Yorkist army. Going south was pointless as all there were to the south were miles of empty wild Pennine moorland. To the east was the city of Newcastle, the Yorkists' base, and to the north were, yet again, miles of open Scottish moors and an almost certain extradition back to England. Ergo, Bamburgh was the only viable option. It was a well-fortified castle on a high bluff with a garrison and almost certainly enough food to withstand a siege until Margaret of Anjou returned with a Burgundian army."

"So, it's off to Bamburgh in the green . . . in the green . . . with the rifles glistening in the sun!"

"What?"

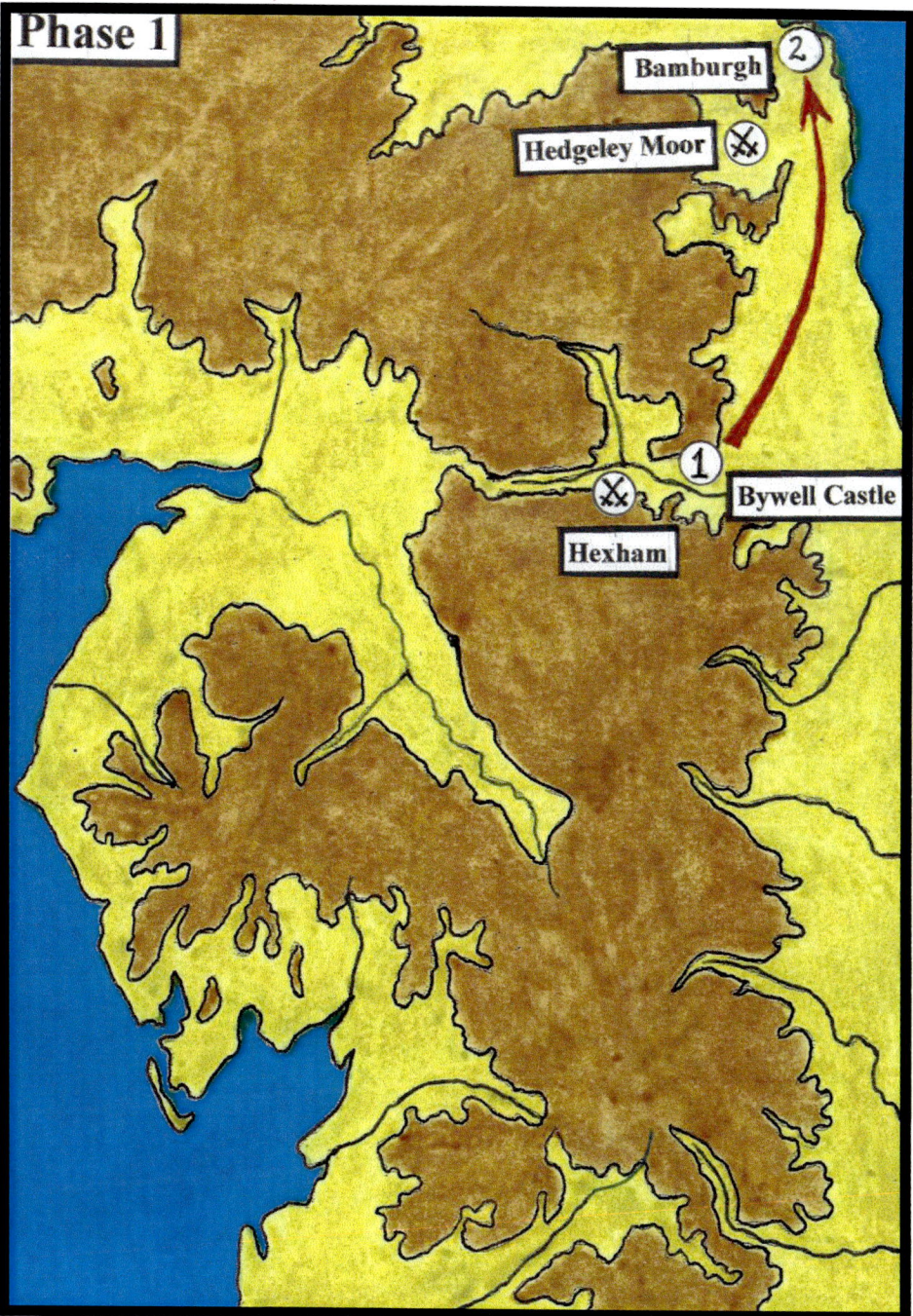

Phase 1

Bamburgh

Hedgeley Moor

Bywell Castle

Hexham

Richard Neville, 16th Earl of Warwick – the Kingmaker.

"Sorry, Yan – I've been listening to some Dominic Behan tracks on my headphones and I just can't get that song out of my head!"

"I'm surprised there's any room in there for anything, brother dear."

"Well, now I understand why Humphrey Neville brought Henry back here to Bamburgh," Yan said, gazing in admiration at the massive fortification of Bamburgh astride a long high ridge overlooking the cold grey North Sea.

Waves lapped on to an almost endless sandy beach below its formidable curtain walls.

"There have been fortifications here for centuries – perhaps for millennia. The Norsemen destroyed one wooden-stockaded structure in AD 993, when it was the Anglian capital of the Kingdom of Bernicia. During the reign of William Rufus the Normans built one of their massive square stone keeps smack on top of the ridge. Over the years, this and that were added to make it even stronger. Eventually, when castles no longer made any military sense, it fell into disrepair. Finally, in 1894 the castle was bought by William Armstrong, the wealthy Victorian industrialist, arms manufacturer and shipbuilder, and it was completely renovated to its current state."

"Yes," Yan mused, "but all that glisters is not gold. The castle, which the refugees from Bywell rushed to in 1464, was not all it seemed to be. Warfare had changed and high-walled forts were no longer as impregnable as they looked. Sieges which used to last months, if not years, soon were to end in no time at all.

"By 1464 the days of trebuchets, battering rams and siege towers were all but over. Gunpowder and cannons had arrived. Although it would take many years to perfect the reliability and firepower of artillery, even those first primitive cannons packed quite a punch."

"So, when the inevitable siege of 1464 wrapped its iron claws around Bamburgh, how long was it able to hold out?"

"As it happened, between two and three weeks!"

"Really?" Tan was aghast.

"Yes, but there were extenuating circumstances; and before we examine exactly what happened, we must stand back and consider a few other factors.

"First things first: we need to understand the mindset of one person in particular – Edward Plantagenet – and probably also that of his best general, Richard Neville, Duke of Warwick. News from John Neville,

Lord Montagu, of the Battle of Hexham must have reached these two by June 1464 – along with the account of King Henry VI's evasion from capture.

"By employing logic to determine the most likely course taken by Sir Humphrey Neville, Edward must have calculated that Henry VI was probably now in Bamburgh Castle. Although John Neville had shown himself more than competent in the art of war, his brother, Richard, was the man to winkle King Henry out of Bamburgh: as recently as December 1462 Warwick had besieged and captured that very fortress.

Warwick must have formulated his assault plans almost as soon as he had been appointed for the task in hand. Messengers were immediately sent post-haste to the Fortress of Calais. He required the following to be shipped immediately to Newcastle: three bombards, two bombardels and as many other cannon as could be spared, along with artillerymen, stone cannonballs, sufficient quantities of high-quality gunpowder for a long siege and transports for the cannons. The specific artillery pieces were named – i.e. the bombards were called Newcastle, London and Dijon, and the bombardels were appropriately called Edward and Richard.

"Warwick certainly meant business, Yan."

"That he did, and he wasn't above using a little psychological warfare too."

"Really?"

"Absolutely! In addition to initiating the siege of Bamburgh on 25 June, Warwick had persuaded the only other two Lancastrian castles in Northumberland to surrender.

"He announced this news to the defenders of Bamburgh, saying, 'Alnwick surrendered two days ago on 23 June, and this very day, 25 June, Dunstanburgh threw in the towel. You should think about doing the same, as after it's all over I intend to execute one soldier for every cannonball fired! As for your commander, Sir Ralph Grey, I will say only this: it doesn't matter what you do – surrender or fight on – your life is forfeited for repeated acts of treason to your king, Edward IV!'"

Tan then enquired, "Did Sir Ralph reply?"

"It seems he couldn't care less and told everyone – including his second in command, Sir Humphrey Neville – that surrendering was not an option."

"And so the bombardment began immediately?"

"Yes, it did, Tan, and as far as one can tell the massed battery was sited on that small hillock to the south of the main gate. Shot after shot hit the walls and keep. Gradually, the massive fortress began to disintegrate into rubble under the constant shelling. Then, as early as the second week of July, an accurately fired missile from the brass bombard Dijon sailed through a window aperture into Sir Ralph Grey's quarters, where he happened to be at the time. A slab of stone was dislodged and fell on the commander's head, rendering him unconscious.

"This was all that Sir Humphrey Neville needed – he immediately surrendered Bamburgh, before Sir Ralph could regain consciousness.

"This, Tan, was the first time in England, apparently, that a castle had been taken entirely by the use of a sustained bombardment by cannons. And before you ask, Sir Ralph was beheaded on 17 July 1464. For unknown reasons, this happened in Doncaster."

"The Kingmaker must have been overjoyed that the capture of Bamburgh had taken such a short time."

"That he was – but not for long."

"Why, Yan?"

"Because despite a thorough search of what was left of the castle, King Henry VI was nowhere to be found – he had escaped!"

"So it was time to get out the thumbscrews?"

"I'm sure Warwick behaved like the true gentleman he was . . . and looked the other way while mere peasants were being tortured. History does not tell us what he learnt, but we do know that within a day or so he and a number of his lieutenants, plus a goodly number of cavalry, headed west into Scotland to the Abbey of Jedburgh."

"Why?"

"Presumably because someone must have told him that was where Henry VI had escaped to."

"So I don't need to guess where we're going to next."

"Oh, I forgot to mention, Tan, that Warwick and his brother had both been ordered to meet Edward IV at Norham Castle, around twenty miles to the north-west and on the English side of the River Tweed, whereas going bu Jedburgh would have clocked up fifty-five miles. As Edward IV wanted their presence to intimidate the young Scottish king, James III, into vacating the English castle, a delay of one to two days might not have been acceptable."

"What happened when Warwick arrived at Jedburgh?"

"It seems he had a fit of pique at not finding Henry VI there either, so he duly ordered his men to trash the place!"

"That Warwick went to Jedburgh on the basis of information gathered at Bamburgh seems logical, as does his reaction at not finding King Henry there. However, what is the proof that Henry went to Jedburgh in the first place?"

"If he did go there, no one knows when he went or who escorted him there. His visit is pure conjecture . . . but, Tan, his going there is the only logical explanation for Warwick's actions and behaviour."

"I agree, but could you try – perhaps – to fill in the gaps?"

"His going to Jedburgh must have been early on in the siege – possibly in the first week of July, when it must have been obvious to everyone that the continued massed barrage of missiles would soon breach the castle walls. As to who specifically might have escorted him there, that too is not known, but certainly it must have been a loyal and trustworthy Lancastrian soldier of rank.

"The escape would have been on a cloudy night, as in Northumberland at that time of year the hours of darkness are quite short. The actual journey to Jedburgh would have been on foot, but why that destination was chosen is not known. It is certainly well to the west of Bamburgh – thirty miles to be exact – and from there Henry could have headed south into England. A religious house might well have been thought of as a safe place, where sanctuary without any questions might be given, especially if the identity of King Henry was not revealed."

Yan and Tan mulled over all of these unanswered questions as Hindenburg III headed towards the ruins of Jedburgh Abbey, once run by Augustinian canons regular. When they arrived the sun was shining and, although the abbey was neither as extensive or as monumentally impressive as Rievault, Fountains, Tintern, Melrose or Furness, its quiet majestic splendour and haunting beauty instilled into our two heroes a feeling of regret that such impressive and beautiful structures were now mere shells of their former selves.

"What a pity!" said Tan.

"Indeed" was all that Yan could muster.

"I was wondering," Tan finally asked, "what do you think happened when one or two English soldiers, with Henry VI in tow, came knocking at the abbey door?"

"It might have been a little awkward at first, but I'm sure whoever was in charge of the group demanded to see the Abbot, who was probably shocked rigid to discover who his unexpected guest was.

"Like Bishop Richard Kennedy, the Abbot probably took pity on Henry VI, but the soldiers were another matter. They were almost certainly asked to leave after being fed and watered. Then, having mulled over what to do next, the Abbot must have formulated a plan which involved sending Henry south to England as soon as possible. But where to? The answer was staring him metaphorically in the face."

"To me it isn't," Tan interrupted.

"To the nearest Augustinian house south of the border – to Lanercost Priory, which was thirty-five miles away. If Henry were robed in black, like all the other Augustinians, and with a hood over his head for good measure, he could have been taken to Lanercost by two priests without anyone suspecting anything out of the ordinary. Naturally, they would have travelled on foot and the Prior of Lanercost must have been warned beforehand to expect three canons at the back entrance of his priory late one evening a couple of days hence."

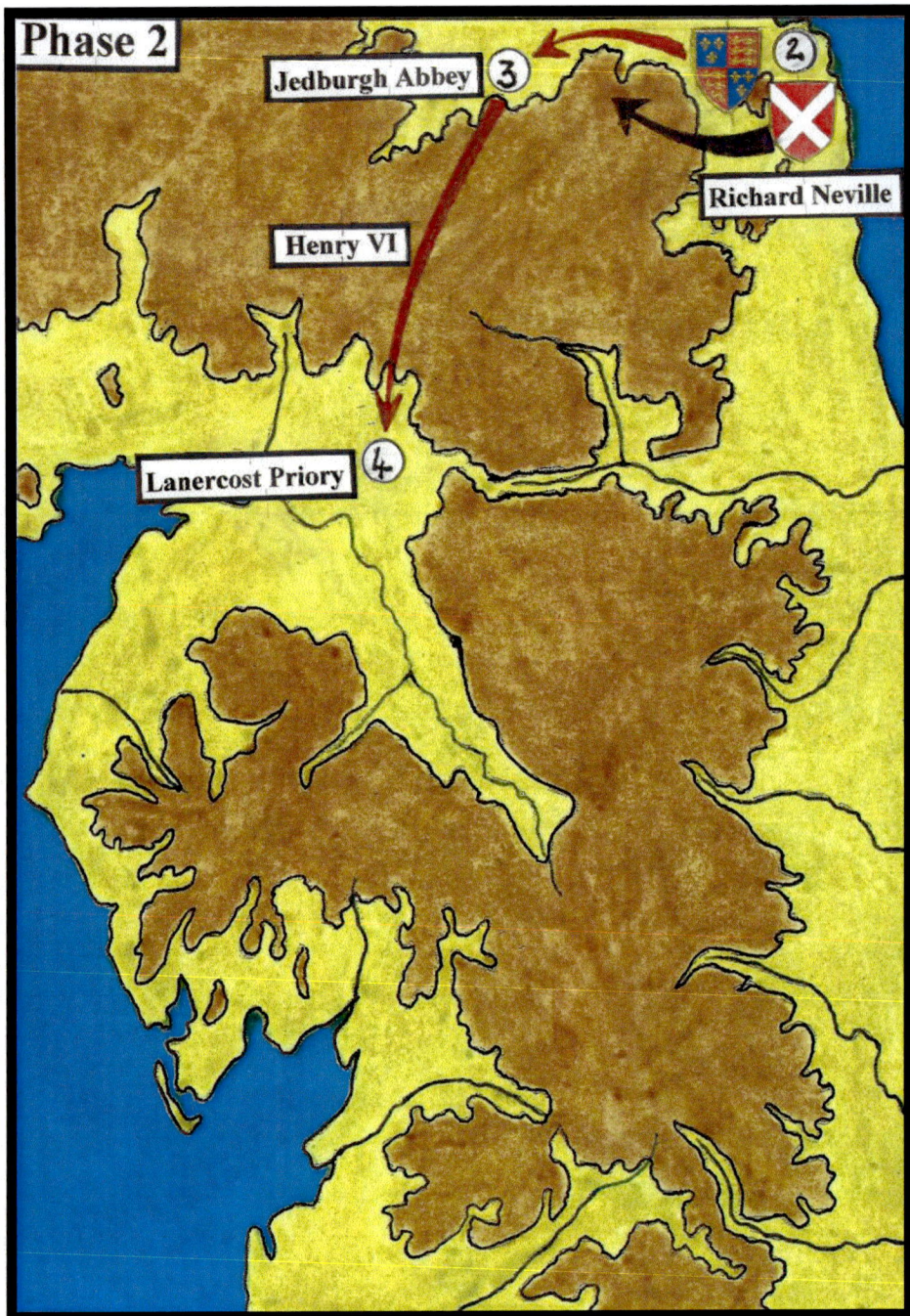

Phase 2

Jedburgh Abbey ③

Henry VI

Richard Neville

Lanercost Priory ④

②

CHAPTER 9 – OH, TO BE IN ENGLAND NOW THAT JULY IS THERE
(Phases 2 and 3)

"You are aware, I trust, that less than three-quarters of a mile south of here is Naworth Castle." Yan alerted his brother to this rather obvious fact as they pulled into the car park of Lanercost Priory.

"So?" Tan responded rather irritably.

"Have a quick look at Frank's two maps of Cumbrian castles and the allegiance of the families or forces occupying them in early 1461 and then again in mid-July 1464."

"Right – I see what you mean. In 1461 Naworth Castle was the ancestral home of the Dacres of the North. Indeed, Randolf Dacre, 9th Baron Dacre of Gillesland and 1st Baron Dacre of the North, died on the battlefield at Towton on Palm Sunday, 29 March 1461. His brother and heir, Humphrey Dacre, also fought on the Lancastrian side that day and was subsequently attainted for so doing. Naworth was then handed over to the Dacres of the South – Joan Dacre, Humphrey's niece, and her husband, Sir Richard Fiennes – who were Yorkists."

"As you can imagine, Tan, Henry VI's arrival at Lanercost must have been a carefully arranged affair, with him being secreted into a cell by the Prior and possibly one other priest. Those who had accompanied him would have been placed in a cell nearby, where they would have stayed until they quietly left on the next dark and cloudy night. It is probable that the Jedburgh canons' return journey would have been on or around 16 July – had they returned to their abbey any earlier, they would have walked straight into the Duke of Warwick and his men, and the game would have been well and truly over."

"A close-run thing, then!"

"Quite so. And another point worth noting is that Prior Alexander Walton of Lanercost would have been reluctant to extend Henry's welcome for too long, as for all he knew there were Yorkists hot on his heels. From all accounts, there weren't; and Warwick himself seems to have lost all interest in the hunt, having drawn a second blank at Jedburgh."

"So, Yan, how long did Henry stay in Lanercost and where did he go from there?"

"I think he stayed there until news arrived from Jedburgh of Warwick's assault on the abbey there, which, being on 15 July, means Henry left the priory on or about the 18th or 19th of that month. One can't be sure, but that's about as near as I can calculate.

"As to his next destination, that could only have been Penrith, a further twenty miles south, where there was a small religious house run by another branch of the Augustinian Order – the Austin Friars. They were mendicant priests who had rejected all forms of strict monasticism for evangelism and a pastoral life of caring for the sick and poor. They lived a somewhat itinerant existence, but had a small central base in Penrith. If Henry had been escorted there in the same Augustinian robes he had worn on his arrival, perhaps with persuasion it might be possible for him to join temporarily their community. Only time would tell if this plan would work."

Henry VI did leave Lanercost and must have safely bypassed Naworth, passing unrecognised in a group of two or three Augustinian canons heading south. There is no reason to believe he didn't arrive at Penrith, but how he fared with these quasi-independent friars is obscured by the mists of time.

The trail Yan and Tan had been following grew cold, so, needing a break, the boys decided to head back to Wiggonby for advice and further information, which their father and Frank Potts would surely be able to supply.

Professor Hardwick was still a little reticent about the whole enterprise, but warmly congratulated them on the progress they'd made.

"You've taken poor Henry Plantagenet 130 miles over a period two months – crossing from Northumberland into Scotland and then south into Cumbria. You've proven to my satisfaction that he must have had help every step of the way. All in all, you've made more progress than anyone else has made in over 500 years. Well done, boys!

"And, by the by, Frank Potts would like to see you. Doubtless he will want to draw a map of Henry VI's travels . . . but he also hinted to me, after the papal helicopter arrived yesterday, that he had information for you – something about a straw in the wind."

"A papal XX-XX Sky-Cruiser landed here?"

Their father knowingly tapped the side of his nose and winked.

They found the ever enigmatic Frank in his beloved library, where years ago he had escaped the far too exciting world of chartered accountancy for a life of tranquillity amongst musty books.

"Morning, Frank," they both said tentatively.

"Is it?"

"It is, and one with a straw in the wind, by all accounts."

"Yes," Frank agreed, lifting up his head. "I've a package here for you from the Professor's old school chum, the now Monsignor Rollo Pecorino Bernardosa, who was seen, according to rumour, recently trying on for size a red hat. Going up in the world, it seems?"

"Really?"

"Yes, and he's currently the second under-librarian to the deputy bookworm in the English Section of the Vatican Library. I'm most envious of him."

"As well you might be, Frank, stuck here in Wiggonby College."

Ignoring the slight put-down, Frank continued: "Anticipating your needing help, I phoned a friend and – hey presto! – this arrived yesterday morning by the papal XX-XX Sky-Cruiser".

"I couldn't resist opening and reading the contents, of course. Inside was a fairly damaged page from a letter sent by Abbot Lawrence of the Cistercian abbey at Furness to a friend – I forget his name – in the Holy City in the year of Our Lord, as he put it, 1464. It's written in a mixture of medieval Latin and Old English, in which you must be a tad rusty."

"Spot on, as ever, Frank."

"I translated the only section of it which was legible. There's little enough to read, but it's better than nothing."

"Thank you, Frank. What does it say?" Tan could hardly contain his anticipation.

"Here, read Frank's translation for yourself."

Met . . . Mach . . . of Crack . . . at the Abbey . . . evening . . . another pilgrim . . . very quiet . . . soft hands and . . . never guess who . . .

"I can't make head nor tail of it, Yan."

"As far as I can work out, Abbot Lawrence met two pilgrims at the abbey one evening in 1464. One was called something like Mach and came from a place whose name began with 'Crack'. He also describes one of the pilgrims as being somewhat withdrawn and having hands not coarsened by manual labour, and hints that his correspondent might be surprised at the pilgrim's identity. . . .'"

"Henry VI!"

"Yes – that's exactly what I thought too, but I wanted to hear it from your lips, to make it sound real."

"We must work out who this Mach was and where he came from. We should ask a friend," Tan said, looking across the room at Frank.

As it happened, Frank didn't know the answer, but said he would give the problem some thought.

"It wasn't that difficult, really," Frank declared rather smugly later that day, hardly able to speak because of the enormously wide grin across his face. "I looked it up on Moogle – the university Internet thingy – and up came Crackenthorpe, a village in what was Westmorland. Ever been there? It's a dump!"

"Yes, we have passed by it."

"The place, where Peg, the Grey Lady, was reburied under a large rock in the Eden?"

"The very one!"

"Would you both like to know who was living in the hall in 1464?" Frank enquired, still beaming widely.

"Perhaps," Tan said grudgingly, not wishing to give Frank an even greater reason to gloat. "Well, go on, then!"

"A father and son who were both called John Machell. The dad was getting on a bit, but the son was apparently in his prime. . . . Oh, and by the by, they were both staunch Lancastrians. Here's a book you ought to read."

"You're doing it again, Tan!"

"What?"

"Singing again, added to which you were also whistling. What is that annoying tune?"

"'We're in the Money', from *Gold Diggers of 1933*. Well, we are in the money, so to speak, and back on track. Stop being so grumpy and tell me what is in the book."

"We could have done with this much earlier, but never mind. Apparently Henry stayed more than once at Crackenthorpe, where he

68

enjoyed the simple life and the pleasures of being their gardener."

"But how did he get there?"

"That is not mentioned and I suspect we shall never know. However, as the crow flies the hall is thirty-three miles south of Penrith and possibly on the far side of the touring circuit of the evangelising friars, who obviously took him in after the canons from Lanercost returned home. Perhaps one of friars at Penrith knew of the political affiliation of the Machells, or even was personally acquainted with someone at the hall. Whatever the case, that person or persons must have recognised Henry and then taken him to Crackenthorpe!

"Henry's arrival at the hall, I've surmised, must have been in early August, but I doubt if his stay lasted longer than a couple of weeks. Appleby Castle is, after all, just three miles down the road and had been crown property since its confiscation from the Cliffords, who also lost both Brough and Brougham after Towton in 1461."

"So while Henry was happily gardening away and under some sort of supervision, in case he strayed too far from the hall, I expect father and son were trying to work out what to do next."

"We do know for certain, Tan, that Henry went to Muncaster Castle, the home of the Penningtons, whom the Machells would have known were 'true-red Lancastrian', unless things had radically changed recently. A messenger sent to the west coast over Wrynose Pass would have clarified that in few days."

"Yes, and although Muncaster isn't exactly in the back of beyond, it is sufficiently off the beaten track to serve as a secure bolt-hole. The nearest Yorkist castle, Millom, the home of the Huddlestons, was ten miles south of Muncaster, but not on the direct route from Furness Abbey, so that shouldn't have been a problem if secrecy was maintained."

"Quite so; and having decided upon the destination, the only remaining questions were who was going to escort Henry there and which route would they take?"

"Well, Yan, the letter clearly indicates the southern route, and his escort can only have been John Machell junior."

"Agreed, and I think they set off on the first step of the journey on or around the middle of September, heading directly for Shap Abbey, a Premonstratensian house, whose abbot was Richard Redman. Their journey of thirty-three miles would probably have taken about four days."

"That's very specific," Tan responded, nearly falling off his chair in amazement.

"Shap is the nearest monastery, and religious houses had, so far, been places, where sanctuary was readily granted – so that's where they must have gone to."

"You've missed out a massively important advantage of going from one priory or abbey to another: being disguised as priests must have been proof against all manner of awkward situations and questions."

"True, but they almost certainly didn't travel to Shap as priests."

"Why do you say that?"

"For one thing the habit of a Premonstratensian canon was white, but the one Henry had worn all the way from Jedburgh was black! He'd have stuck out like sore thumb, and young Machell even more so as he probably didn't possess a habit of any colour."

"Yan, I know you've worked it out, so tell me in what disguise could they have travelled to Shap without being stopped by anyone?"

"I'm surprised you have to ask, Tan. Why, as lepers, of course!"

Phase 3

Jedburgh Abbey

3

Richard Neville

Henry VI

4

Lanercost Priory

5

Penrith Austin Friars

6

Crackenthorpe Hall

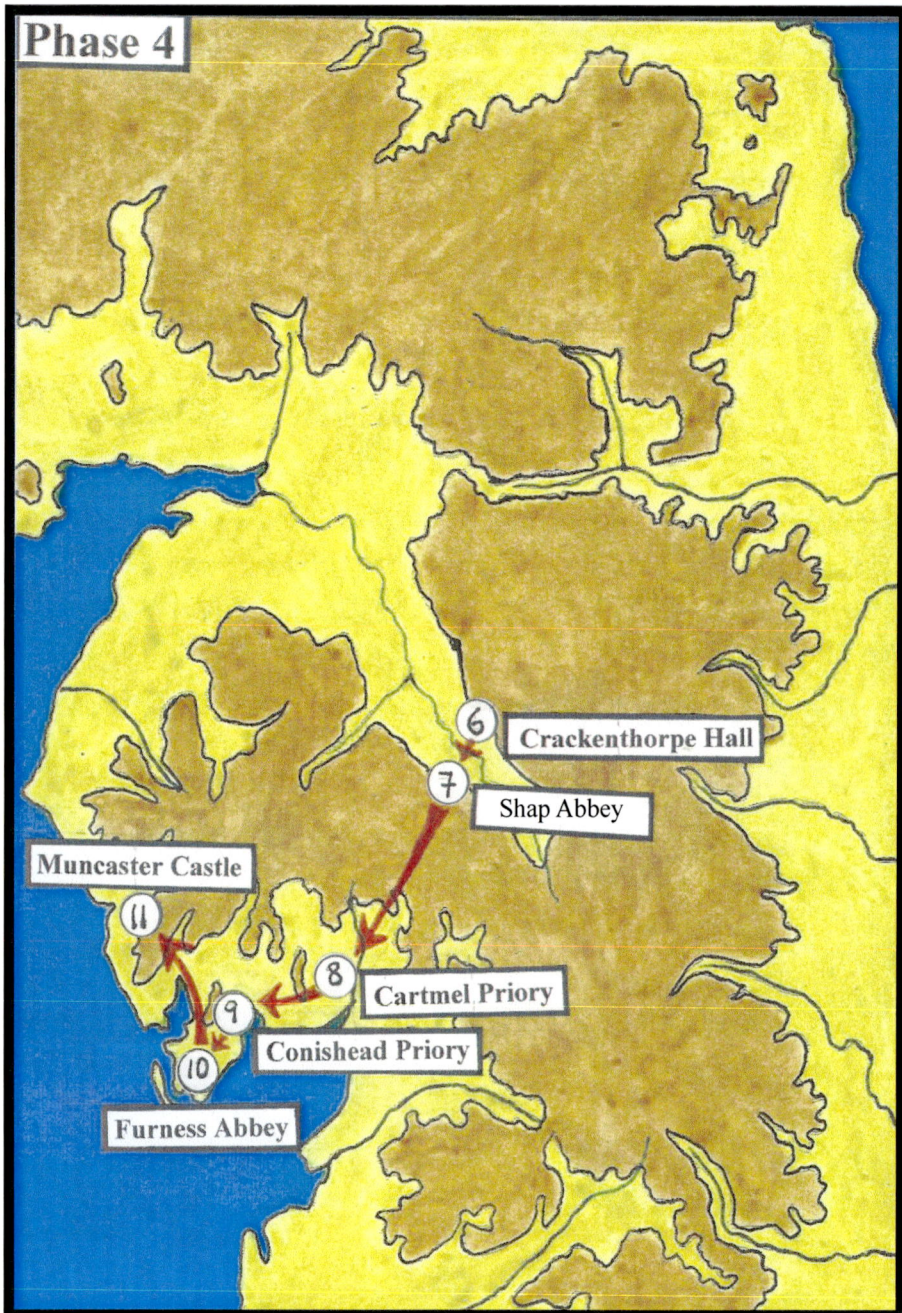

Phase 4

Crackenthorpe Hall

Shap Abbey

Muncaster Castle

Cartmel Priory

Conishead Priory

Furness Abbey

CHAPTER 10 – FOR WHOM THE BELL TOLLS
(Phase 4)

"Yes, Tan, you heard me correctly. I believe that John Machell and Henry VI, dressed up in dirty, torn hooded gowns tied at the waist with a knotted and frayed cord, swathed in soiled bandages over their hands, feet and faces and each carrying a roughly hewn bell-topped staff, limped their way from Crackenthorpe Hall to the Premonstratensian Shap Abbey . . . as lepers.

Not only would such a disguise have virtually guaranteed their not being stopped, but, as lepers, they might not have been too out of place in that part of Westmorland. Quite simply, Shap Abbey had in the past (between 1223 and 1246) managed a leper hospital, or lazaretto, in Appleby called St Nicholas.

On nearing the abbey, they might have disrobed, buried their ragged outer garments and donned clean ones. With the addition of a hat bearing a scallop shell, and the removal of the bell from their staffs, they would have then been completely transformed into pilgrims."

"I like it, Yan, and it could have worked."

"On arriving at the abbey, John Machell would have sought an audience with the abbot, Richard Redman, who incidentally would eventually become not only the head of his Order in England but also Bishop of Ely. There would have been no need to reveal Henry's true identity – just a simple request for food and shelter overnight, as well as permission to visit the abbey church."

"And the next day?"

"It was on to Cartmel Priory, where another community of Augustinian canons regular lived, worked and prayed – just another thirty miles to the south-west. It was now nearing the end of September. The nights would have been drawing in and getting cold – perhaps a little too chilly for Henry to be sleeping out. With that in mind, John Machell might have appealed to Prior William for a week's lodging, saying that his companion was not in the best of health. He might also have delivered a fictitious verbal message of greeting from Prior Alexander of Lanercost, as all Augustinian houses would have been communicating with one another after the Jedburgh incident."

"And then?"

"It would have entirely depended on whether Henry's identity had been discovered, or it may even have been revealed by John Machell. It's unlikely that anyone in the priory would have known what Henry VI looked like, but Machell might have wanted a change of costume – Augustinian robes for the journey to Conishead, the sister priory of Cartmel. He may not have identified Henry by name, but might have suggested that, so dressed, he could not be mistaken for the old king – thus he would avoid being roughly treated.

It was only eight miles to Conishead – the shortest stretch so far – and would have only taken a day. After another week's rest, they could then have tackled the next thirty miles to Furness, arriving by mid-October. After that another thirty miles to Muncaster Castle dressed as pilgrims. Taking into account a few days in Furness, they would have arrived, say, in early November."

At this point Frank Potts delivered a message from their father, who wanted to see them.

"Well, you two have been busy," he said. "Oh, and I wonder what you make of this," he added, pointing at the stamp on the package in which the letter from Monsignor Bernardosa had arrived.

"It's just an English stamp," Tan observed.

"Delivered in a helicopter from Rome? I think not."

"You mean—?"

"It was delivered by the Royal Mail. We were tricked. I telephoned Rollo to thank him and it turns out the papal XX-XX Sky Cruiser had been grounded all week due to technical problems. What we saw was another illusion, just like all the other spectacular displays."

"So Henry VI wasn't taken to Furness Abbey after all?"

"No, that part was true. Frank was able to find a reference to his visit, but the letter was a forgery. I think you were being nudged in the right direction by someone – any idea by whom?"

"Yes, but no proof, as you well know," Yan said wearily.

"Well, be that as it may, I really don't think there's any reason for you two to duplicate John Machell and Henry VI's southern trip from Crackenthorpe to Muncaster Castle."

"I was looking forward to seeing Tom Fool's portrait in Muncaster Castle," Tan said disappointedly.

"Well, you can't, because Muncaster is still closed due to Lockdown. I went there last year and heard the story of Tom Skelton of which there are many versions. I took some photos and even bought a tee-shirt!

I'll get Frank to bring in some tea – it's about that time in any case. Over tea and Cumberland rum-buttered crumpets I'll tell you all about it – including what happened when those two weary travellers finally arrived at their destination."

"Firstly, here's something I picked up online – basically a chronicle called *The Machells of Crackenthorpe*, which seems to indicate that John Machell senior died in the autumn of '64, while his son was escorting Henry VI all the way to Muncaster. So when they arrived Sir John Pennington not only would have welcomed his king, but would also have taken John Machell junior aside to break the sad news. Doubtless, the new squire of Crackenthorpe would have bade farewell to his king and headed home the next day.

I think, additionally, he may have promised to return in the spring to escort him back to Crackenthorpe. Henry, as we know, stayed there more than once and this would have been how that was accomplished."

"And now I shall tell you the story of Tom Fool, or Tom Skelton, of Muncaster. I shall give you the pukka version – the one recounted by Wilson Armistead in his book *The Tales and Legends of the English Lakes* – plus a few observations and additions of my own. However, I must warn you that the best description of all these stories is – and I hesitate to tell you this – what everyone avoids standing in when walking across a field full of bulls."

This was greeted by a chorus of guffawing, which Tethra waited to die down before relating the legend.

"As far as I can tell, it all started on 1 May 1484 with the annual dance around the maypole erected beside Devoke Water, a large tarn about a mile north of Muncaster Castle. All the maids and young men were decked out in their finery – the girls especially so, with garlands of flowers on their heads and fine leather shoes on their feet.

"The local villagers and shepherds watched and probably cheered them on. Then, unexpectedly, a beautiful young woman whom no one recognised arrived on the scene dressed as a shepherdess. She sadly attracted the attention of a lout called Will the Wild from Whitbeck, a village twelve miles to the south, who demanded not just that they dance together, but that she also gave him a kiss. She rebuffed Will, but readily agreed to partner a carpenter's son called Richard.

"Will's anger knew no bounds and he resolved to be avenged on the pair. His discovery that the maid was none other than Helwise Pennington, the daughter of Sir Alan Pennington of Muncaster Castle, prompted him to approach Sir Ferdinand Hoddleston, the lord of Millom Castle, who, it was well known, wanted to marry her. Sir Ferdinand was livid when he heard from Will the Wild that an upstart peasant had been so intimate with the 'love of his life'. The boy had to be taught a lesson, and Sir Ferdinand knew the very person to teach it: Tom Skelton, or Tom Fool, the jester of Muncaster Castle.

"Tom Skelton appears not only to have been a sociopath, but also a serial killer on the side. He liked to tell visitors of safe routes across the Esk Estuary, then watch them drown in quicksand. Naturally, he agreed to help Sir Ferdinand, for three silver pennies, and then chopped off Richard's head with his father's axe while the boy was napping.

"No one profited by this murder, and Tom wasn't suspected of having committed the crime. Helwise went into a Benedictine covent on Soulby Fell near Pooley Bridge and Sir Ferdinand went off to war, dying on Bosworth Field fighting for Richard III on 22 August 1485 – but not before leaving sufficient money, should he fall in battle, to pay for masses to be said for his and the carpenter's son's soul."

"A really good story!" Tan said with gusto.

"That is exactly what it is – total fiction. There were two Penningtons called Alan, but they lived in the fourteenth century – and no trace of a Helwise Pennington can be found anywhere. As for Sir Ferdinand, there's no trace of him either. A Richard Huddlestone did die in 1485 – but not at Bosworth. His claim to fame was that he married Richard Neville's illegitimate daughter, Margaret – oddly enough around 1464–65. Then there's Tom Skelton – he did exist and was the servant/tutor of Lord William Pennington. However, he is thought to have lived from 1620 to 1668."

"Well, that does put a slightly different complexion on the story," Tan admitted. "But didn't you say you had taken some photos of Tom Fool's portrait?"

"I shouldn't have taken them really, but I did. I also used a flash – just as the tour guide ordered the window curtains to be pulled back for dramatic effect. I forgot to get the film processed until last week . . . and here are the two pics I took."

Yan and Tan nearly fell off their chairs and Tethra became almost apoplectic when the snapshots were revealed. Tan then brought out his smartphone and lay it alongside the colour prints so as to compare them with the picture he'd taken of the Loki Stone at the Parish Church of Kirkby Stephen.

Tom Fool, or Tommyrot.

?

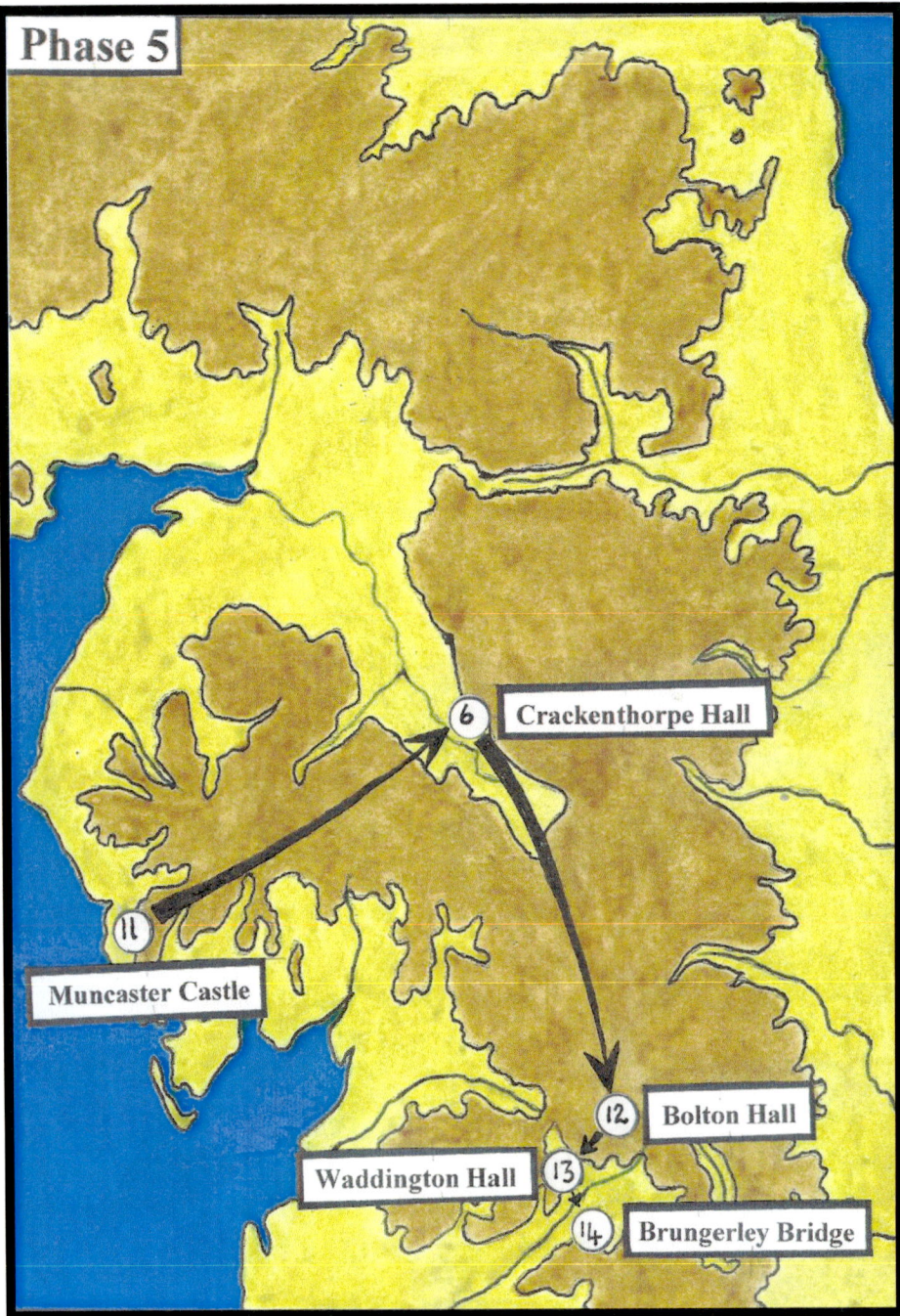

Phase 5

Crackenthorpe Hall

Muncaster Castle

Bolton Hall

Waddington Hall

Brungerley Bridge

CHAPTER 11 – A FINAL THROW OF THE DICE?
(Phase 5)

"Well, Yan, that was a turn-up for the books – seeing Loki's head on Tom Fool's shoulders."

"It was . . . but not entirely unexpected when you think of it. Maybe that's who Tom Fool was all along!"

"You may well be right. Anything connected with him is bound to be . . . well, suspicious to say the least. And I'm not entirely sure we've done with him ourselves yet. But with regard to Henry VI's magical mystery tour, that's nearly over."

"Well, it isn't quite. Henry VI, when we left him, was tucked up in Muncaster Castle and the year was still 1464."

"Do you think John Machell really went back for him in the spring of 1465?"

"Yes, I do. It just seems exactly what a man of his calibre would have done."

"So, Yan, when the snows had melted on the tops and the old Roman road over Wrynose and Hardknott Pass to Galava (Ambleside) was open – say in the first week in April 1465 – John Machell and his servant, 'Enry, would have travelled eastward on horseback to Crackenthorpe."

"Yes, I think that is exactly what they did. Clearly there were no search parties out looking for King Henry VI, so it would have been safe for them to lodge in inns along the route."

"Naturally, they would have had to carefully skirt south of the old fort of Brocavuum (Brougham Castle) and then head down the road on the east bank of the Eden to Crackenthorpe, which they would have reached by mid-April at the latest."

"How long do you think Henry stayed there before moving on?"

"You can't keep a good gardener down, Tan, so maybe by late May or early June it was time for him to move on."

"But why on earth didn't he just stay there in total obscurity? The Yorkist regime probably thought he was dead in the Pennines or somewhere in the Lake District."

"Who knows? But move on he did, heading east into West Yorkshire and then finally into North Lancashire, but as for who accompanied him . . . ? Mayhap John Machell took him on the first leg, but after that . . . ?"

"What happened next, Tan, is pretty scant, but in early July Henry VI visited the home of the Pudsay family at Bolton Hall in Bolton-by-Bowland in West Yorkshire. There's still a well there which he apparently divined – it's called King Henry's Well. In gratitude for his hospitality, Sir Ralph Pudsay was given a fine pair of brown Spanish boots lined with deer skin, a pair of gloves and a spoon."

"A bit like the glass bowl Sir John Pennington received."

"Quite so. Then it was on to Waddington Hall in North Lancashire – about a mile north of the River Ribble and Clitheroe. This was the home of Sir John Tempest, who, unlike his brother, Sir Richard Tempest of Bracewell, was a staunch Lancastrian. Another guest at the hall was a rather sinister fellow who went by the name of William Cantlow, or the Black Monk of Abingdon. This fellow apparently recognised Henry Plantagenet and informed John Tempest. The latter promptly set in motion a raid on the hall by Yorkist supporters.

"This took place the next day, 13 July, just as King Henry, Sir Richard, John Tunstall and Thomas Manning, the former Dean of St George's Chapel at Windsor (until 1461), were about to dine. A violent struggle ensued and John Tempest's arm was broken by Tunstall, who aided King Henry to escape on horseback.

"The two didn't get far – only to a site now known as Brungerley Bridge, on the outskirts of Clitheroe. There they were apprehended by the injured John Tempest, Thomas Talbot and Sir James Harrington of Horby – for which they all received 100 marks expenses and a bounty of £100.

Henry was kept prisoner in Clitheroe Castle overnight, then sent south the next day, under guard and on horseback with his feet bound to the stirrups. They covered the next 245 miles in ten days and Henry was turned over to his old adversary Richard Neville, Duke of Warwick, at Islington on 24 July. The wheel of fortune had truly turned against poor Henry Plantagenet.

He was held prisoner in the Tower of London for the rest of his life – apart, of course, for the period between 3 October 1470 and 11 April 1471, when he briefly regained his throne. He ended his days there too – murdered in his cell on the night of 21 May 1471 after his seventeen-year-old son, Prince Edward, had been dragged out of Tewksbury Abbey, after the battle of that name on 4 May that same year, and dispatched summarily into the next life.

The Lancastrian dynasty was over – though young Henry, Duke of Richmond, was to claim two extremely tenuous royal links through his mother, Lady Margaret Beaufort. She was firstly the great-granddaughter of John of Gaunt, the son of Edward III; secondly, and even more tenuously, her husband was Edmund Tudor, the son of Owen Tudor and Catherine of Valois, whose first husband had been Henry V."

"What complicated lives some people live!" Tan mused.

"And what a brutal time the fifteenth century was. It's just as Cersei Lannister said: 'When you play the Game of Thrones, you either live or die!'"

"Now, that's a cheery thought, Yan."

The next day Yan, Tan and their father, Tethra, all met up to discuss the whole affair from beginning to end.

"And what are you boys going to do next, now that it's all over?"

"I'm not sure, Fatha," Yan intoned.

"Well, I for one am not ready to return to Mungrisdale. I'd like to take a trip to Brungerley Bridge and see where King Henry VI's magical mystery tour finally came to an end."

"I'm up for it too . . . if Hindenburg III is available."

And it was.

Brungerley Bridge.

CHAPTER 12 – A BRIDGE OVER TROUBLED WATERS

"So this is the famous Brungerley Bridge, where King Henry VI was finally captured on 13 July 1465 after evading his enemies for over a year," Tan Hardwick mused.

"Well, yes and no," Yan replied. "This bridge was only built in 1816; in 1465 people crossed the Ribble just above this point, either by the ford at low water or by Hippings, or large stepping stones."

They stood there for a while leaning over the bridge, staring into the dark waters slowly passing beneath the arches with only the odd swirl to break the silence of a totally peaceful afternoon.

Tan nudged his brother and pointed at an image forming beneath the surface.

"What on earth is that?" he whispered.

"Can't you guess?" Yan replied.

"I thought you'd like to see the face of my 1465 persona – Ye Blacke Monke of Abyngtone, as I was once called," said a voice that had materialised out of nowhere. "Well done! You've come up with by far the best solution of any I have heard so far. I couldn't have done any better myself."

With that, Loki's face slowly merged into the depths of the Ribble and drifted downstream towards Morecambe Bay, out of sight of man, sheep and all other species – at least for the time being.

THE APPENDICES

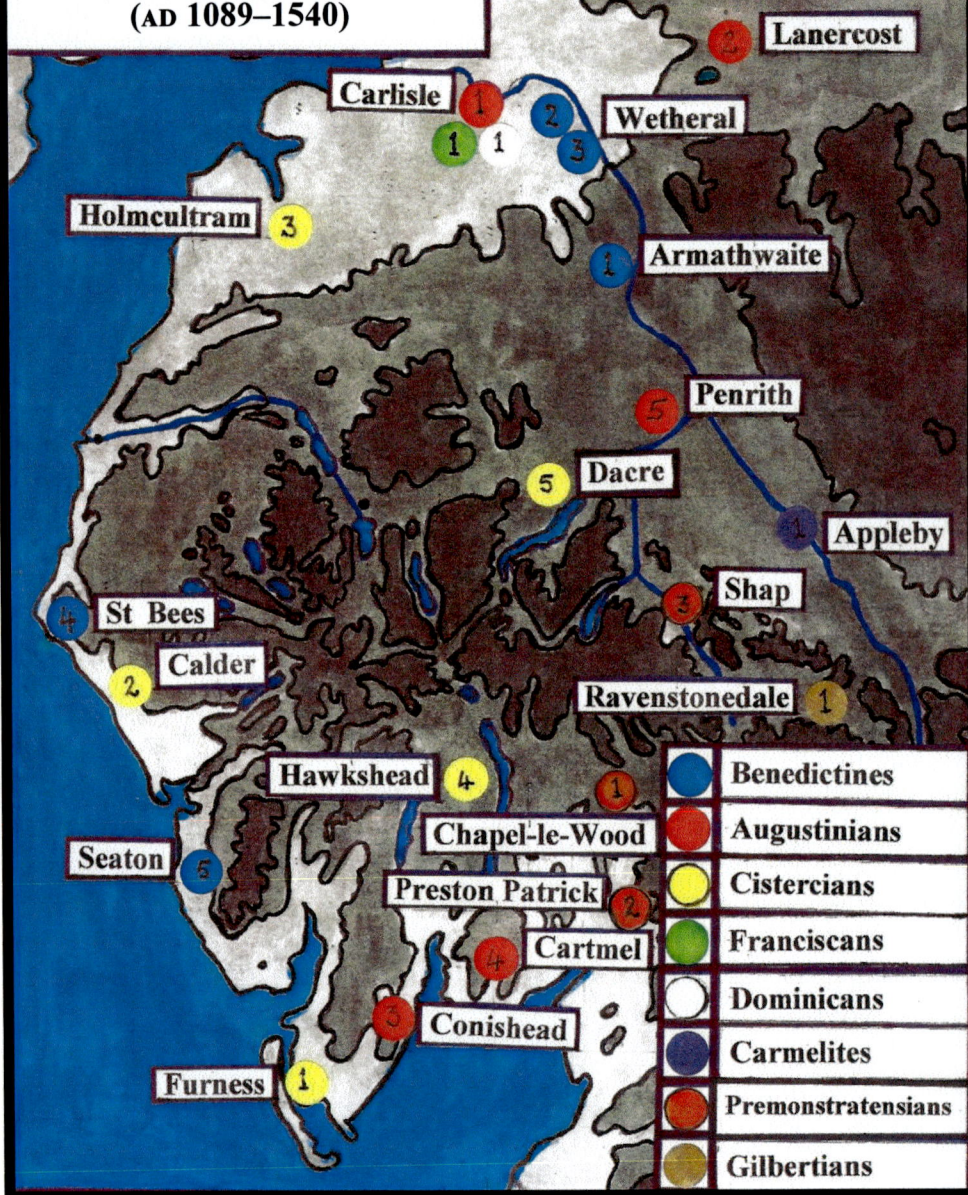

Monasteries in Cumbria
(AD 1089–1540)

Lanercost

Carlisle

Wetheral

Holmcultram

Armathwaite

Penrith

Dacre

Appleby

St Bees

Shap

Calder

Ravenstonedale

Hawkshead

Chapel-le-Wood

Seaton

Preston Patrick

Cartmel

Conishead

Furness

Benedictines	
Augustinians	
Cistercians	
Franciscans	
Dominicans	
Carmelites	
Premonstratensians	
Gilbertians	

APPENDIX 1: MONASTERIES, PRIORIES, ABBEYS, FRIARIES AND NUNNERIES
(Key to Map on Page 49)

Benedictine
1. Armathwaite Nunnery (1089–1539).
2. Wetheral Priory (1106–1538).
3. St Constantine's Cells (1112–1538).
4. St Bee's Priory (1120–1539).
5. Seaton Priory (Nunnery) (1190–1537).

Augustinian
1. Carlisle Cathedral Priory (1122–1540).
2. Lanercost Priory (1160–1537).
3. Conishead Priory (1188–1536).
4. Cartmel Priory (1189–1536).
5. Penrith Austin Friars (1291–1539).

Cistercian
1. Furness Abbey (1123/24–1537).
2. Calder Abbey (1134–1536).
3. Holmcultram Abbey (1150–1538).
4. Hawkshead Grange (1160–1537).
5. Dacre Abbey (1145–1539).

Franciscan
1. The Greyfriars of Carlisle (1233–1539).

Dominican
1. The Blackfriars of Carlisle (1233–1539).

Carmelite
1. Appleby Friary (1281–1539).

Premonastratensian
1. Chapel-le-Wood (1192– ?)
2. Preston Patrick Abbey (1192–1200).
3. Shap Abbey (1199–1540).

Gilbertian
1. Ravenstonedale Priory (1200–1539).

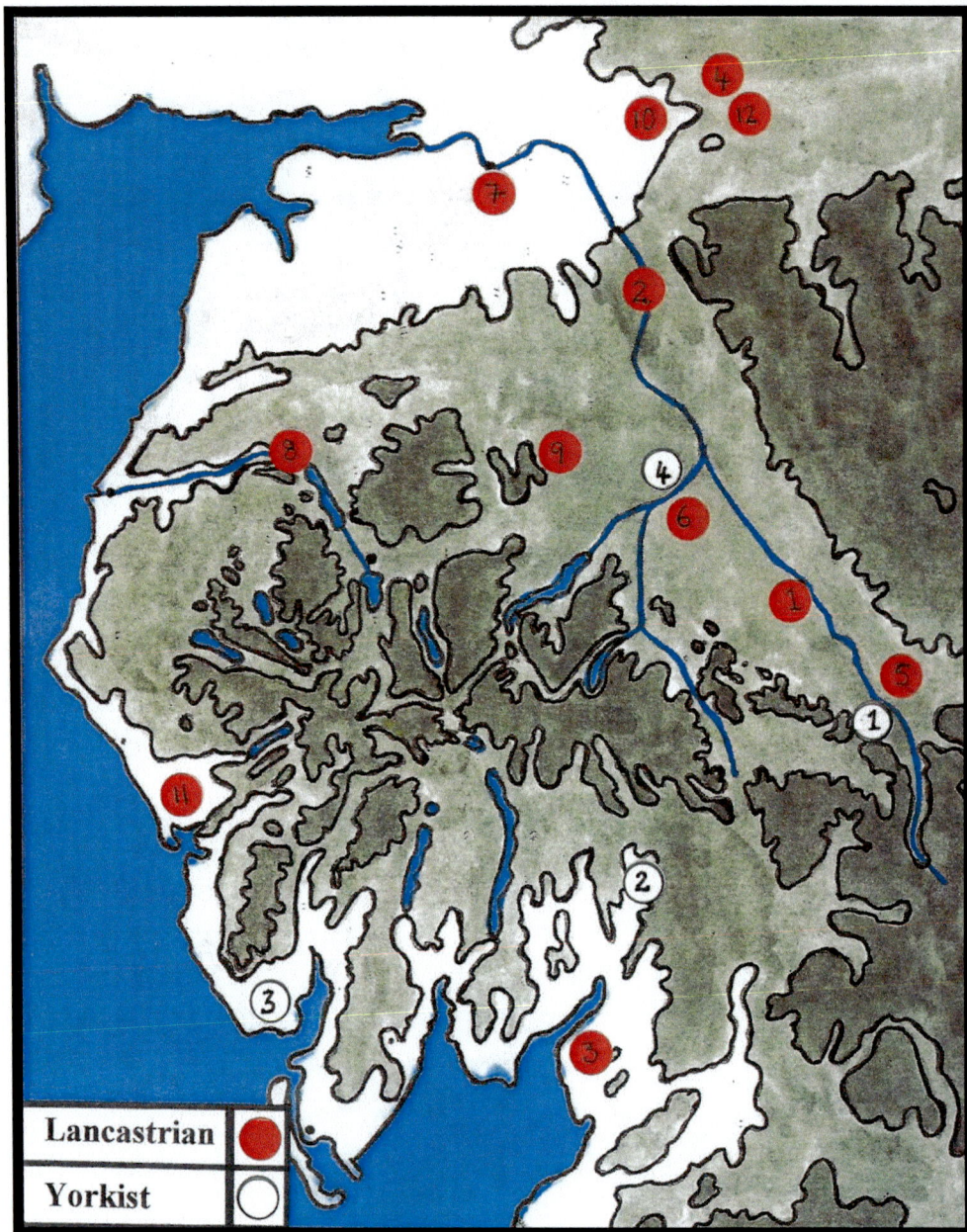

Cumbrian castles – pre-Towton (1461).

APPENDIX 2: CUMBRIAN CASTLES –
PRE-TOWTON (1461)
(Key to Map on Page 40)

Lancastrian
1. Appleby = Clifford family.
2. Armathwaite Castle = Skelton family.
3. Arnside Tower = Lord Hungerford.
4. Askerton Castle = Dacres of the North.
5. Brough Castle = Clifford family.
6. Brougham Castle = Clifford family.
7. Carlisle Castle = royal castle (Henry VI).
8. Cockermouth Castle = Percy family.
9. Greystoke Castle = Greystoke family.
10. Irthington Castle = Dacres of the North.
11. Muncaster Castle = Pennington family.
12. Naworth Castle = Dacres of the North.

Yorkist
1. Hartley Castle = Musgrave family
2. Kendal Castle = Parr family.
3. Millom Castle = Huddleston family.
4. Penrith Castle = Richard Neville (Warwick).

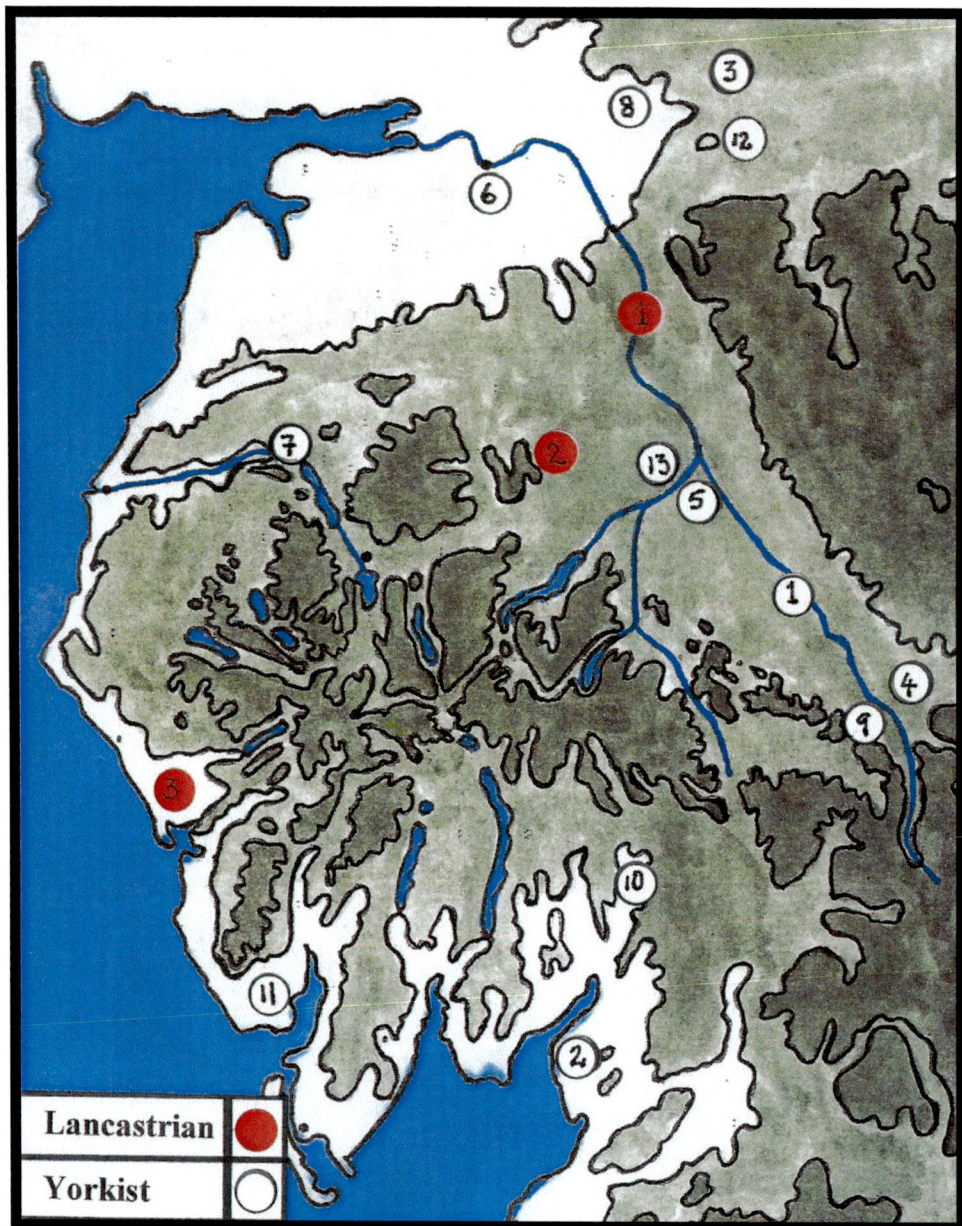

Cumbrian castles (1464–1465).

APPENDIX 3: CUMBRIAN CASTLES
(1464–1465)

Lancastrian
1. Armathwaite Castle = Skelton family.
2. Greystoke Castle = Greystoke family.
3. Muncaster Castle = Pennington family.

Yorkist
1. Appleby = Crown property (Clifford family, Lancastrian before Towton in 1461).
2. Arnside Tower = Crown property after Hexham.
3. Askerton Castle = Crown property (Dacres of the North, Lancastrian, before Towton in 1461).
4. Brough Castle = Crown property (Clifford family, Lancastrian, before Towton in 1461.)
5. Brougham = Crown property (Clifford family, Lancastrian, before Towton in 1461).
6. Carlisle Castle = royal castle (Edward IV).
7. Cockermouth Castle = (formerly belonging to the Percy family, but now probably Crown property).
8. Irthington = Crown property (Dacres of the North, Lancastrian, before Towton in 1461).
9. Hartley Castle = Musgrave family.
10. Kendal Castle = Parr family.
11. Millom Castle = Huddleston family.
12. Naworth Castle = Dacres of the South (Dacres of the North, Lancastrian, before Towton in 1461).
13. Penrith Castle = Richard Neville, Earl of Warwick (originally Yorkist; Lancastrian from 1460).

ROMAN CUMBRIA

APPENDIX 4: ROMAN CUMBRIA

The Wall Forts (from West to East)

1. Bowness-on-Solway – Maia. This fort was dedicated to the mother of Mercury by Jupiter. It was the most westerly fort, and was known as the 'Larger Fort'.
2. Drumburgh – Congavata.
3. Burgh-by-Sands – Aballava, 'An Orchard'.
4. Carlisle – Luguvalium, 'The city dedicated to Lugus', a deity in the Celtic pantheon.
5. Stanwix – Uxelodunum or Petriana, 'The Waterside Fort', was a large cavalry fort on the north bank of the Eden (or Itouna) opposite Luguvalium.
6. Castlesteads – Camboglanna, 'the fort near the winding valley'.

Other Outpost Forts (from North to South)

1. Beckfoot – Bibra.
2. Old Carlisle – Maglona Carvetiorum.
3. Caermote – Caermote – a Roman auxilliary fort.
4. Old Penrith – Voreda. The Roman name is possibly related to *veredus*, a courier's horse or waystation, which in turn may be related to the Celtic word *gorwydd*, a horse.
5. Maryport – Alauna, 'the beautiful place' (of the Carvetii). The River Ellen derives its name from Alauna.
6. Papcastle – Derventio Carvetiorum, a *vicus* or civilian settlement. The River Derwent and Derwent Water derive their names from Derventio.
7. Burrow Walls – Magis.
8. Brougham – Brocavum.
9. Moresby – Gabrosentum.
10. Beckermet – Tunnocelum or Iuliocenon, the site of a suspected fort and port.
11. Hardknott – Mediobogdunum.
12. Ambleside – Galava.
13. Low Borrow Bridge = ?

14. Ravenglass – Glannoventa, 'the market on the shore'.
15. Watercook – Alavana.
16. Burrow-in-Lonsdale – Calacum, 'the flower basket'.
17. Lancaster – name unknown.

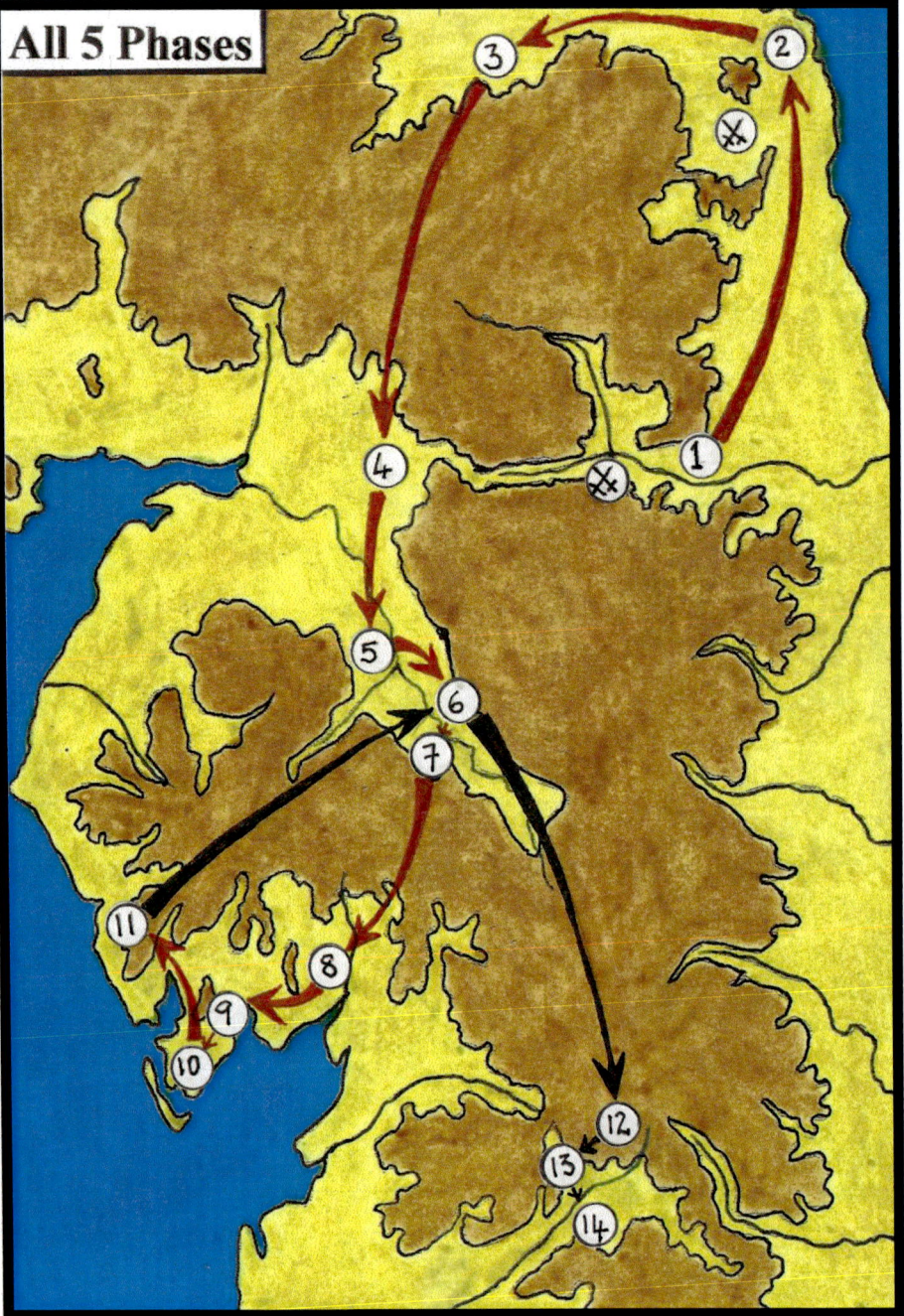

All 5 Phases

APPENDIX 5: HENRY VI'S JOURNEY –
ALL FIVE PHASES

- Bywell Castle (1) to Bamburgh Castle (2)   45 miles.
- Bamburgh Castle to Jedburgh Abbey (3)   33 miles.
- Jedburgh Abbey (Augustinian) to Lanercost Priory (4)   35 miles.
- Lanercost Priory (Augustinian) to Penrith Austin Friars (5)   20 miles.
- Penrith Austin Friars (Augustinian) to Crackenthorpe Hall (6)   10 miles.
- Crackenthorpe Hall to Shap Abbey (7)   33 miles.
- Shap Abbey (Premonstratensian) to Cartmel Priory (8)   30 miles.
- Cartmel Priory (Augustinian) to Conishead Priory (9)   8 miles.
- Conishead Priory (Augustinian) to Furness Abbey (10)   30 miles.
- Furness Abbey (Cistercian) to Muncaster Castle (11)   30 miles.
- Muncaster Castle to Crackenthorpe Hall (6)   45 miles
- Crackenthorpe Hall to Bolton Hall (12)   50 miles.
- Bolton Hall to Waddington Hall (13)   5 miles.
- Waddington Hall to Brungerley Bridge (14)   1 mile.

BIBLIOGRAPHY

Battles in Britain (1066–1547) by William Seymour – Sidgwick and Jackson (1975).

The Best Kept Secrets of the Western Marches by H. G. Wills – Arthur H. Stockwell Ltd (2015).

The Canticle of Rollo Pecorino Bernardosa by H. G. Wills – Arthur H. Stockwell Ltd (2020).

The Castles of England by Frederick Wilkinson –Letts Guides (1973).

Discovering Castles in England and Wales by John Kinross – Shire Publications (1973).

Edward IV by Jeffrey James – Amberley (2017).

English Battlefields by Michael Rayner – Tempus (2004).

Fatal Colours by George Goodwin – Phoenix (2011).

Ghostly Cumbria by Rob Kirkup – The History Press (2011).

The Ghostly Guide to the Lake District by Tony Walker – Vellum (1998).

Henry VI by Bertram Wolffe – Yale University Press (1981).

In the Eye of Storms by H. G. Wills – Arthur H. Stockwell Ltd (2017).

Margaret of Anjou by Helen E. Maurer – The Boydell Press (2003).

Margaret of Anjou by Jacob Abbott – Forgotten Books (1902).

The Medieval Fortified Buildings of Cumbria by Denis R. Perriam and John Robinson – Cumberland and Westmorland Antiquarian & Archaeological Society (1998).

North-Eastern England during the Wars of the Roses by A. J. Pollard – Clarendon Press, Oxford (1990).

Room 22 Revisited by H. G. Wills – Arthur H. Stockwell Ltd (2016).

Squires, Knights, Barons, Kings by William E. Baumgaertner – Trafford Publishing (2009).

Tales and Legends of the English Lakes by Wilson Armistead – Simpkin, Marshall & Co. (1891).

Warwick the Kingmaker by Charles W. Oman – Lector House (1916).

Warwick the Kingmaker by A. J. Pollard – Hambledon Continuum (2007).

The Wars of the Roses by Dan Jones – Penguin Press (2014).